Open the Unusual Door

True Life Stories of Challenge, Adventure, and
Success by **Black Americans**

Open the Unusual Door

True Life Stories of Challenge, Adventure, and Success by **Black Americans**

Edited and with an introduction **by Barbara Summers**

Graphia

An Imprint of Houghton Mifflin Company • Boston 2005

Other Graphia Titles:

I Just Hope It's Lethal: Poems of Sadness, Madness, and Joy
edited by Liz Rosenberg and Deena November

**Zen in the Art of the SAT: How to Think,
Focus, and Achieve Your Highest Score**
by Matt Bardin and Susan Fine

Lost in the Labyrinth
by Patrice Kindl

A Certain Slant of Light
by Laura Whitcomb

Story for a Black Night
by Clayton Bess

The Fattening Hut
by Pat Lowery Collins

Zazoo
by Richard Mosher

For Kimson

Acknowledgments

I am profoundly grateful to all the authors who gave permission for their memoirs to be included in this book.

For their practice of easy access to untold numbers of lives and stories, I thank the public library system, especially the libraries in Teaneck, Englewood, and Hackensack, New Jersey, and their helpful staffs.

For their insightful editorial guidance, I thank Eleni Beja, Emily Linsay, and Melissa Dobson. I also thank my intrepid agent, Michele G. Rubin, for her patience and resilient good humor.

For keeping their hearts and doors open way beyond the call of friendship's duty, I thank Leah Colette Clendening and Charles F. Harris.

And for being an extraordinary public school teacher for thirty-five years, I respect and admire my sister, Lucy Summers.

For information about permission to reproduce selections from
this book, write to Permissions, Houghton Mifflin Company,
215 Park Avenue South, New York, New York 10003.

www.houghtonmifflinbooks.com

The text of this book is set in Minion.
The illustrations are by Gina Triplett.

Library of Congress Cataloging-in-Publication Data

Open the unusual door: true life stories of challenge, adventure, and success by
Black Americans / edited by Barbara Summers.
    p. cm.
  ISBN 0-618-58531-1 (pbk. : alk. paper)
  1. African Americans—Biography—Juvenile literature. 2. Successful
people—United States—Biography—Juvenile literature. 3. Adventure and
adventurers—United States—Anecdotes—Juvenile literature. 4. Self-
confidence—Anecdotes—Juvenile literature. I. Summers, Barbara, date.
  E185.96.O64 2005
  920'.009296073—dc22

                                                                    2004028230

ISBN-13: 978-0618-58531-1

Manufactured in the United States of America
HAD 10 9 8 7 6 5 4 3 2 1
A list of permissions appears on page 207.

Contents

Introduction • ix

The Welcome Mat

Barbara Summers

Before the great writer James Baldwin knew he was a writer—and *long* before he became great—he had the good fortune to meet an artist, a painter, a man who saw something in his young brown face that made him want to open the door and invite Baldwin inside. Walking through that door changed Baldwin's life, opened it up to all sorts of experiences he had never imagined. Baldwin recounts how this painter, Beauford Delaney, often sang *Lord, open the unusual door.*

Whether to let someone in or walk through it oneself, at some point in life we all face an unusual door. Even the people behind the famous names in this book.

The artists and athletes, the scientists and entrepreneurs, the thinkers and doers, who speak in this collection all faced challenges and made choices. Many were very young at the time. Antwone Fisher was born in prison and spent his entire youth without a home to call his own. Dexter Scott King was only seven when his famous father was assassinated. Russell Simmons was sixteen when he almost shot a man, not in a rap song but in real life.

Of course, not all of the storytellers here were so young

when they faced a door or a difficult passage or, simply, the blank unknown. And not all serious challenges must involve life or death. They don't have to be loud and explosive to be dramatic or life-changing.

Sometimes the choice is a quiet one. Like the choice Neil deGrasse Tyson made at age nine to make the study of the stars his life's work. After his first exciting visit to the Hayden Planetarium, his eyes were opened to the majestic night sky in a way that made him never stop wanting to learn more.

Sometimes the challenge comes from an argument with someone you can't beat, someone like Mother Nature. Dangerous, stormy weather arose just when Michael Cottman, a scuba diver, tried to reach back through time to an ancient sunken slave ship.

But then sometimes the challenge comes from a debate you have with yourself. Like the understanding Whoopi Goldberg struggled to reach when her fourteen-year-old daughter announced that she was pregnant. What Whoopi wanted for her daughter was not what her daughter wanted for herself. And yet, the fundamental issue was choice—Who decides? And how? And what are the consequences?

What all of these people experienced—in one way or another—required them to look hard at the changes they wanted and needed to make in order to better their lives. They had to open up to new ways of thinking, doing, and living. That is why their stories are gathered here as examples of challenge and choice.

Even I have a story to add. When I started putting this collection together, I read dozens of memoirs by interesting people. Deciding on the final list was tough. I felt almost as if I had to choose between my best friends. How would they feel if they were rejected? How would *I* feel if it happened to me? I soon found out.

One of the people I wanted to include was Dr. Benjamin Carson. Dr. Carson is a world-renowned neurosurgeon who specializes in healing children. As a child himself, though, he had a vicious temper and a bad attitude toward schoolwork. How he turned around, with the help of his dedicated mother and teachers, made for an unusually happy ending. I *had* to have a piece of his book to put in the one you're holding in your hands right now. Turns out, that wasn't possible. I felt a little sad. He did, however, invite me to talk face-to-face with him at the Johns Hopkins Hospital in Baltimore. I felt much better.

If you haven't heard this lesson before, hear it from me now: When one door closes, another one opens.

I don't know about you, but a hospital is a place I like to visit as rarely as possible. Still, once inside, I navigated the long hallways, finally pushed open the door to Pediatric Neurosurgery, and shook hands with Dr. Carson. Instantly I forgot that these hands were the same ones that had tried to stab another kid when he was a teenager, and now performed the miraculous surgery that separated Siamese twins, removed brain tumors, and saved lives.

I knew that he would be making rounds shortly and that we had no time to waste. He knew what I was after and got right to that point in his early life when he had to make a choice:

"I was a person who thought he had a lot of rights. The more rights you think you have, the more someone is going to infringe on them. It got me thinking that when you get angry and lash out, the person most likely to be hurt is you. *You* hurt yourself. I began to recognize that it's not a matter of what rights you have or don't have. It's a matter of what opportunities you have.

"One of the things that happened after the stabbing incident—from that day till this—I started reading the book of Proverbs every day. There's an awful lot of wisdom there. It says stuff like a person who can listen is wise; a person who cannot listen is a fool; and a fool is always right in his own eyes. I said, That sounds just like me. I said, You're a fool, and you need to figure out how *not* to be a fool. I kept reading and reading, and I realized that what I needed to do was listen, listen to people who've already been through it, because many times they had to learn the hard way. You don't *have* to learn the hard way."

Profit from others' experience. Keep learning. Strive for excellence. Achieve academically. These are some of the things Dr. Carson emphasized in his talk with me. When I closed the door to his office in the hospital I felt strengthened in my resolve to put together a book as rich and inspiring as I could.

What happened next?

That's the question that drives all stories forward, and the ones in this anthology are no exception. Each story is told in a different way, just as each life is lived in a unique way. But all the authors share something in common: a willingness to open the door to readers. They invite us in to tell us what happened to them and what they did to make things happen. They let us see who they are, what they think, and how they feel.

So consider this introduction a welcome mat, and open the unusual door. You might be letting in a stranger who becomes a good friend. Or you might be letting yourself out to face a brand-new world. Either way, you can't lose. What are you waiting for? Go ahead. Open it.

DEREK JETER *wears number 2 on his New York Yankees uniform, but to many fans he is number one. Since 1995 he has helped the Yankees reach the World Series six times and win the Series four times. A gifted athlete, his steady focus, hard work, and passion for baseball made him a leader and eventually captain of the team. In 1996 he established the Turn 2 Foundation which funds college scholarships and provides leadership and antidrug programs as well as baseball clinics. Although Jeter earned $15 million in 2003, he is careful to insist that* he *makes the money; money doesn't make him.*

Rookie

I remember sitting in my hotel room on a warm evening in July in Tampa, Florida, feeling antsy. It was too warm to stay inside the room. Besides that, I had too many questions swimming through my mind about where I was and what I was doing.

So I ventured out onto the balcony. I watched the cars buzzing by. I counted the cars, counted how long it took for the light to turn from green to red. I did anything to keep me from focusing on baseball. I don't know how long I was out there, but I didn't get any answers right away.

I couldn't escape from baseball. I felt like I had already failed. I had been playing with the Class A Tampa Rookie League team for about a week and it had been torturous since I failed to get a hit in my first 14 at bats. I stood on that balcony and questioned myself. Had I made the right decision in signing a professional contract at eighteen? Of course, everyone would say. You were the sixth pick of the draft and the first high school player selected, you were fortunate to go to the team you cherished, and you received a signing bonus of $800,000. How could I possibly think of that as a mistake?

But the money wasn't helping me much as I stood there watching cars and doubting myself. I could have attended the University of Michigan on a baseball scholarship, and I would have spent my first year playing baseball and hanging out in a dormitory room with no pressure on me. My toughest decision probably would have been whether to get pepperoni or sausage on my pizza. Instead, I felt like I'd never felt before in my life. Lost.

I had imagined being in this hallowed position for over a decade, wearing a Yankee uniform, earning a paycheck from the Yankees, and playing baseball every day. I knew it was going to be an adjustment from high school to pro baseball, but I hadn't expected to feel as overwhelmed as I did. I hadn't imagined that I'd wind up crying in my hotel room night after night because I was playing so poorly.

When I got to the rookie league team in the Gulf Coast League, I was late so I missed the first two weeks of the season. I was even late for my first game. The players took the fifty-two-mile ride from Tampa to Sarasota on a crowded bus that day. I must have looked like a prima donna when I hopped out of the air-conditioned car of the vice president of player development, with a duffel bag over my shoulder. The Yankees didn't let me play on that first day, a day when the main thing I learned was to stop tilting my cap back on my head like I was a big man on campus. As a Yankee, you tugged the cap down tight over your brow to look neat and professional.

I just watched, said hello if someone said hello to me, and tried to get acclimated. The nightmare started the next day, when I went 0 for 7 and struck out five times in a doubleheader. I also made a throwing error on a grounder up the middle that caused us to lose one game. I had struck out just once in 59 at bats during my senior year of high school, so you can imagine how I felt. I felt like going home that very first day. Could someone erase this day from my life and let me start over?

As much as my family was prepared for me to leave, the finality of it still caught us by surprise. My sister Sharlee was about to become a teenager, and she was mad at the Yankees for taking me away from her when she knew that she would need an older brother the most. My mother was concerned because I didn't know how to iron or how to cook and I had to live on my own. I was leaving, and if everything proceeded as planned, I would be gone for good.

My father drove me to the airport the day I departed. I got on that plane with a lump the size of a golf ball in my throat, and the only thing that prevented me from crying was thinking I might see someone I knew.

Even though I had been voted the finest high school player in the country and was the first high school player drafted, I'd come from Kalamazoo, Michigan, and the talent level there was not nearly as rich as it is in many of the warm-weather states. We only played about two dozen games a year, and we played lots of doubleheaders to take advantage of any decent weather we had. If a pitcher threw 85 miles per hour in Kalamazoo, he was considered untouchable. In rookie ball, everyone threw harder than that. The pitches looked like Tic Tacs. So I wondered if I was really as good as everyone had predicted, and that's what brought me out to the balcony on that warm night.

I had doubts. I felt like I was overmatched in everything. The whole game seemed like it was moving in fast-forward. The mound seemed like it was 80 feet away, instead of 60 feet 6 inches. The throw from shortstop to first base felt like I was throwing it from center field to home plate. It seemed like everyone else was on Rollerblades while I was slogging through quicksand. I was us-ing a wooden bat, not aluminum, for the first time, and that was an adjustment.

I still think that the rookie league is one of the toughest leagues any player ever has to conquer. The games in the Gulf Coast League were played in sweltering ninety-degree heat throughout Florida and there are very few spectators. If you're not doing well, and I wasn't, you can let those dreary elements get to you.

I always liked to play in front of crowds as a kid. My mother used to say it was like I was on Broadway. I would try on my uniform the night before a game to see how I looked in it. I did that from Little League through high school, parading around my house like I was a model on the catwalk. Now, a few weeks after I had forty scouts at some of my games, I was playing in the pros and there might be as few as a dozen people there. It shouldn't have bothered me, but it did.

I could have really disintegrated in rookie ball. I could have crumbled and never recovered. But I kept getting positive reinforcement from the Yankees and from my parents. The Yankees have an organizational rule that they will not alter anything a player does in his throwing, hitting, fielding, or running until he has been with the team for at least thirty days. They don't want young players to show up and feel like everything they have ever done is incorrect. They do it to help build and maintain confidence.

I think it's a smart approach, and I think it helped me work through my problems. Even though I was struggling, I didn't have coaches berating me for what I might have done wrong. When I was trying to establish myself, I wanted to feel as though I was making progress and doing something worthwhile. My statistics stunk, but I didn't lose all of my confidence.

I have to give them credit for their strategy. They worked hard to keep me focused on what I was doing well and explained why I was still pretty good at some of the things I hadn't mastered yet. I think that's a great approach for everyone, not just baseball players. If you can remember one or two positives from your pursuit of a certain goal, you'll begin each day with confidence.

It's hard to overlook mistakes, and we shouldn't ignore them, because we can learn from them. But when you're really toiling, you need to find those shreds of optimism and cling to them. The Yankees saw me as a long-term investment, the way a good teacher would notice a potentially stellar student during his freshman year. The teacher shouldn't worry if the kid has a little trouble in his freshman year because the goal is to equip him to make it to college by the time his four years are up.

The Yankees didn't talk about my batting average much in that first year. They told me that I had a nice feel for the barrel of the bat, that I was being selective, and that I wasn't totally fooled by breaking pitches. They liked my habits and my approach and told me that no one would ever remember what I batted in my first year.

The Yankees started me at Class A Greensboro in the 1993 season and that felt more like the big leagues to me because we'd have a few thousand people at every game. I was there at the start of the season and that made a difference, too. I did well offensively, hitting .295 with 5 homers and 71 RBIs.

But I just couldn't get comfortable on defense. By the third week, I was hoping that no one would ever hit another grounder to me. My footwork was lousy; I was bobbling balls before I could make plays; and I was trying to do too much with my arm.

The Yankees took computer images of me fielding, slide-by-slide snapshots of what I did at shortstop. I was doing things that I didn't even realize. Those images really opened my eyes to the work I needed to do. Sometimes I fielded a grounder and tapped the ball against my glove before throwing to first, losing valuable time. I was like a seven-foot center who doesn't realize that he dribbles the ball after grabbing a rebound, instead of taking it right back up and dunking.

You have to want to improve. We all know what we can and can't do, and it's up to us to try to eliminate whatever weaknesses we can. Be honest with yourself, tell yourself how you need to improve, and then work on making those improvements.

When you go into a situation expecting to succeed, whatever good happens shouldn't surprise you. I don't think I'm being cocky when I act that way. It's just the mentality that I have. You should always think that you're going to be successful and you should always want to be successful. If it doesn't work out for you and you strike out with the winning run on third or you fail your driver's test, you have to acknowledge that something went wrong, and adjust your actions and go after it again the next time. The next time you try that task, don't think about the time you faltered. Think about all of the times in which you have excelled. That's the path back to success.

One of the more disappointing things you can do to yourself is not even try to do something because you're afraid of failing. Maybe you want to design clothes or run marathons or work in Europe for a year. Don't shy away from it, because ten years from now you will be asking yourself if you could have done it. That's why I work so hard now—because I don't want to question whether I could have done more with my career when it ends. I'm never going to put myself in a position where I wish I could have done more. We control what we do with our lives. Don't be afraid to use that control to make things happen.

Everyone wants to be known as a big-game player in professional sports. When I come to bat in a pivotal spot, I want people to say, "Uh-oh, here he comes." That's the way it was with Michael Jordan and that's the way it is with Tiger Woods. If you plant that seed in someone's head, it's one more thing for them to think about while they're trying to beat you. I'm always confident because I know I've done well before so I expect to do it again. If a pitcher senses that I'm confident, it works to my advantage.

This strategy can help you in any walk of life. You have to want to show everyone that you're good, even great, at what you do. For me, the important things in my life are baseball and trying to remain the same person I've always been. For you, it can be anything. Just have a passion for what you're doing.

QUEEN LATIFAH *changed her name from Dana Owens when she broke into hip-hop, adding a strong female voice to the male-dominated mix. She challenged lyrics and attitudes that insulted women. By bringing her sassy self-confidence to the fore, Latifah emphasized the importance of self-knowledge and self-respect. When a tragic event tested her core values, she fought her way back to strength. She expanded her award-winning singing career into producing and acting. In television and movies, Queen Latifah has developed into a proud, full-figured, full-fledged star.*

A New Attitude

The music was the lure. Funky beats I had never heard before, brash words spoken in rhyme. Kids—dressed in fly sweat suits, baggy jeans, and the latest sneakers—danced in the center of the floor, surrounded by crowds forty and fifty deep. And onstage at any given night—Grandmaster Flash, Dougie Fresh, Eric B. and Rakim, Salt-N-Pepa, the Beastie Boys, Run-D.M.C., MC Lyte. This was the Latin Quarters, the mecca of hip-hop in the mid-1980s. And I was right there in the thick of it all, taking it in.

This was my education in the world of rap. For my mother, it was Excedrin Headache number 9. I was definitely too young to be going to New York City all alone and hanging out all night. Looking back on it, I say to myself, "What were you thinking?!" I was blinded.

But in truth, I do know what I was thinking. Immediately, I was one with this world. My blood beat to its beat. Not only did I want to be there, I *had* to be there, and nothing was going to stop me.

Rap was the newest music. Overnight, it seemed, rap had become the common language of youth. But it wasn't just music.

It was an expression, a culture, an attitude.

When I came onto the scene, rap was entering a new phase, with KRS-One, Public Enemy, and the Jungle Brothers. The consciousness movement was emerging. It was not just simple rhymes over the most popular songs; the music was about saying something.

Hip-hop transcended ethnic and racial lines. Young people were getting the chance to voice their opinion, and everyone—from the kids around the way to the mainstream public to the big white men at the record companies—was paying attention to it. And simply by being there, I was one of the people making the culture. It was amazing to be a part of such a force.

The Latin Quarters was on the corner of Forty-eighth Street and Broadway. It doesn't exist anymore. When I was coming up it was vintage Times Square, with its funky movie theaters, peep shows, Playland, fake-ID shops, shady characters, and danger. I ate it up.

The Latin Quarters wrote the bible of hip-hop for me. I would bring the music, the vibe, the dances back to East Orange, New Jersey, and to Irvington High. Every night, through the Lincoln Tunnel, I was transporting clothing styles and a new lingo that turned out to be more than a passing fad: a dialect that still sticks.

In charge of activities at Irvington High School, my mother was responsible for getting DJs for the class parties. One day she introduced me to Mark the 45 King. He was from the Bronx, where rap began, and he was a master on the turntables. Mark and I hit it off right away. I started hanging out with his boys after school in his basement in Irvington. That was Jersey's Rap Central, where everybody was writing rhymes and trying out over Mark's mixes. At first I sucked. But I knew I had it in me. I could hear in my head the way I wanted to sound. It was just a matter of getting it from my brain to my voice.

Mark's basement was always buzzing with people from the neighborhood—and eventually we became a posse. I was the only female MC in the group and the youngest, so I called myself Princess of the Posse. Down there the world was far away and time ceased to exist. We were about the music. Only the music.

The Burger King on High Street in Newark gave me the money to afford my hip-hop education. We'd all meet at Burger King on Saturdays after I got off, around 11:00 PM. In the bathroom, I would change out of my ugly brown, orange, and yellow outfit and into my hip-hop gear—a Swatch sweat suit, a pair of K-Swiss sneakers, some scrunchy Guess socks, a Benetton fisherman's hat, and either my Benetton or Swatch backpack.

I was geared down; you couldn't tell me nothing. When the Burger King clothes came off, I put on a whole new attitude. My brother had saved up for a nice gold rope chain, and we would alternate wearing that one chain. But I would never wear it to the city. I saw too many people get their chains snatched, either on the train or in the club. I basically played it cool and watched.

It seemed like everyone wanted to be a rapper.

Ironically, though, I wasn't really thinking about a record deal. I was content to do my thing in Mark's basement. It was a hobby. I had my sights set on college. That's how I was raised. I ended up going to Borough of Manhattan Community College, where I studied broadcast journalism. I wanted to be a newscaster or a lawyer. Communicating, whatever the form, was my thing.

Hip-hop showed me another way to communicate, another way to reach people, another way to state my case.

I was sitting in the kitchen of our apartment in East Orange. I was flicking between WBLS (107.5 FM) and WRKS-Kiss (98.7 FM). It was the summer of 1987, and DJ Red Alert on 'BLS and Marley Marl on Kiss had one of the best over-the-music battles going. We used to tape their shows, they were so good. So I'm chilling in the kitchen, and I hear the beginning of "Princess of the Posse."

My record. My song. Me. Playing on the radio. I was so excited. I just ran to the window and screamed out, "My record is on the radio! My record is on the radio!" I'm sure I woke up half the neighborhood. But I didn't care. I hadn't even officially signed with a label. And they were playing my song on the radio.

Becoming Queen Latifah and being a famous rapper wasn't my only goal. I also wanted to make enough money so that my family would never want for anything. By the time I was twenty-two, I was very close to that goal. I was able to afford a house, cars, clothes—and the kind of lifestyle we could only dream about as kids.

But even with a career that took me all over the world, making money, and making music that people were responding to, something was missing. I would go on tour, be back in town for a couple of days, and never get a chance to see my mother and brother.

I decided I would buy a house and we would all move back in together. I missed renting movies with my brother Winki and my mom. I missed our family dinners that were full of laughter. I missed waking up in the morning and having breakfast with them before the craziness of the day started and we all went our separate ways. Although Winki and I were grown and had independent lives, I wanted us to be under the same roof.

I finally found a house. The frame was there, the stairs were finished, and the woods enclosed the backyard. But it was just an open house without amenities. That was perfect for me. I got to create and design the inside. It was contemporary and had great angles, skylights, and a big deck. And it was big enough for all of us to have our own space. I couldn't wait for us to move in. Between Winki's boys and my crew, the house would be alive all the time. We would have fun—and we would be a family again.

Not more than a month later, Winki was gone.

The last thing in the world I thought I would be doing was picking out my brother's casket. It was silver, with a white lining so soft it looked like clouds. Winki looked strong in it, wearing his police uniform. But his hands were cold. His eyes were closed. This was the most painful moment of my life. I loved him so much that I didn't want to live.

My brother was twenty-four. Dead? What are you talking about? It wasn't getting through.

Winki's death tested me. When we were riding our mo-
torcycles around East Orange, I took our togetherness for
granted. I felt immortal. I knew that what you have one
day can be taken from you the next—I knew it in my
head, but I didn't feel it yet in my heart. Why should I?
Until the night I saw Winki's mangled bike in the hospital
parking lot, I had never confronted loss. That night, I
found an inner strength that I didn't know I had. I resisted
it, because I just wanted to curl up outside the hospital
and disappear.

But that inner strength was stronger than despair.
That's what living means—facing the music—whether it's
bad luck and bad attitude, failure, disappointments—or
the death of the young man who was your brother and
best friend. And living means letting go.

You have to let it go, or else you're going to go with it.

It came right back to the music. When Winki died, the
song in me died. But I had obligations to fulfill. You have
to handle your business, no matter what you're going
through. In this case, my business was making music. And
it was a blessing. For most of my life, music has been my
pathway to peace.

I rarely mention drugs in my music. I don't want any
business glorifying the fast lifestyle that a lot of rappers

promote. Yes, I experimented—and I came close to losing control. I was lucky—and I saw others who weren't. That's why I have chosen to make my music about being grounded, about treating yourself as royalty.

We always have an "it won't happen to me" attitude when we see other people making mistakes. Don't be fooled. It can happen to you—if you aren't careful, if you don't know who you are—anything can happen.

Lesbian.

That word seems to follow me lately.

I'm not afraid to do roles like Cleo, the hard-core, from-the-'hood, down-and-down dyke in *Set It Off*. I worked that role and I played her to a T. It was one of my most challenging parts. But it seemed that when that movie came out, everyone wanted to know, "How much of Cleo is really you?"

There's still all kinds of speculation about my sexuality, and quite frankly, I'm getting a little tired of it. A woman cannot be strong, outspoken, competent at running her own business, handle herself physically, play a very convincing role in a movie, know what she wants—and go for it—without being gay? Come on.

I want people to see me as someone who is proud and

comfortable with who I am. I'm a liberal-minded woman who couldn't care less what anybody else does in their bedroom. That's on them.

I don't act the way society dictates that a woman "should." I am not dainty. I do not hold back my opinions. I don't stay behind a man. I'm not here to live by somebody else's standards. I'm defining what a woman is for myself. Simply put, I am not interested in subscribing to what society has decided for half of humankind. I am an individual, and this is what I know. I don't like being a victim. I don't like being weak. I've been to those dark places. And never will I go back to them. It's a fool who doesn't learn from mistakes. A queen uses her mistakes as a stepladder to climb higher.

And I've had a long way to climb.

Growing up, I was uneasy about my body. It was big. People look at me now and think, "Wow, there's a full-sized woman who has it together." Puh-lease! It took me years to get to the point where I love my body. And I do truly love my body. But I had to go through stages. I hated my breasts. I hated my butt. I even hated the way I walked. Some girls, with no effort, can just walk cute and ladylike. Not me. I had this lumbering stride. I used to practice and practice, but I still couldn't fix my walk. So I said, "Fughetit!" I had to accept myself, walk and all.

When you define yourself based on what you like, who you are—and the body and mind that God gave you—people eventually catch up. You don't have to change to fit anybody's preconceived notions. But it's hard to do that when the image that assaults us is a lie. More than 80 percent of people in this country are overweight. That's a reality. But 99.9 percent of what we see and what we want is that supermodel/movie-star body that gets the gorgeous clothes, the stylin' jewelry, and that wins the man. So the majority are trying to fit their square peg into a round hole.

Find that square hole and fit in where you fit in.

I'm about being healthy. I'm about feeling good at whatever size I am. Watch what you eat and be healthy. But don't try to fit into an image. Do it because *you* want to.

I have had so many people slap images and labels on me. People have expectations of who they think I am or who they think I should be. But I am not just the outer covering that people see. I don't have to wear a sign that says I AM QUEEN LATIFAH for people to treat me with respect. I command it. And I don't need Queen Latifah to be a queen. All I need is to be myself.

SUSAN FALES-HILL *is an award-winning television writer and producer. Her mother was Josephine Premice, a spirited actress, dancer, and international chanteuse who was born in Haiti and raised in the United States. Susan Fales was born in Italy and lived there with her family for several years. When they relocated to New York City, Fales moved in a sophisticated, multicultural world carefully crafted by her glamorous mother. She used her own experiences to enrich pioneering TV shows featuring successful middle-class African Americans.*

Semper Fabulous

"*This family isn't black,* they're Jewish!" the fifty-something executive exclaimed over my shoulder as I viewed an episode from *The Cosby Show*'s first season in the Viacom conference room. I hardly knew this man; he worked on the syndication side of things, and I as a writer's apprentice. Yet here he stood telling me that the Huxtable family had no counterparts in reality. I sat for a moment speechless and stunned by the double-barreled assault of his arrogance and his ignorance. I then calmly asked him what he meant.

"Look at them," he answered, agitated, "she's a lawyer, he's a doctor, they live in that . . . house!"

To follow his logic, there were no black dual-career couples and black people did not live in townhouses. Period. His statements echoed newspaper reviews that criticized the show for creating a fiction and refusing to address the plight of the urban underclass—clearly the first duty of any and every situation comedy about black people. I didn't recall anyone leveling that accusation at *The Jeffersons*, perhaps because George Jefferson posed no real threat to our country's power structure. He might have "moved on up to the East Side," but with his rough-hewn ways, he wouldn't be movin' on up to the country club, the corporate boardroom, or the designer-decorated boudoir of a socialite trophy wife anytime soon. The Huxtables, on the other hand, could give any upper-middle-class white person a run for their money. Therein lay the danger.

"There are plenty of families like this," I told the critic, remembering the blacks in Sag Harbor, Long Island—a summer retreat of the black bourgeoisie—where you couldn't walk for more than a few feet without running into a black person with a minimum of two advanced degrees. "My mother grew up in a house just like that. In Brooklyn, in the thirties and forties," I informed him. I envisioned my grandparents' second-floor parlor with its grand piano, a VanDerZee assortment of elegantly dressed black people gathered for Sunday tea, and Aunt Adèle and Josephine's concert on piano and violin.

This middle-aged white man had the audacity to tell me that such scenes did not exist. He dismissed my statement with a wave of his hand, shook his head as if to say, "You don't know what you're talking about," and walked away. In such moments, I always wished I could import family members and school friends—black men and women from the Lycée or Harvard who'd gone on to distinguished careers as architects, investment bankers, entrepreneurs, reporters—as visual aids to prove my point.

My mother and her coterie of black friends in the acting profession had prepared me for such myopia. Growing up, I sat through many a Dom Perignon–soaked postmortem held by my mother in the wake of auditions for which she and several of her female friends had been called and then rejected because they were judged insufficiently "down home," "urban," or "maternal." Translation: they didn't fit a white producer's image of "typical black womanhood."

Whose black home had these television, commercial, or movie producers visited, anyway? My mother and her friends often wondered. What "typical black women" did they know, other than their housekeepers and the occasional assistant?

But it was useless to preach to the ignorant. My mother, beautiful blue-eyed Ellen Holly, Carmen de Lavallade, the former prima ballerina with the caramel coloring and deportment of a Madagascarian queen, earthy Rosalind Cash, elegant Jane White, and majestic Gloria Foster would often lose roles to women who more closely resembled Aunt Jemima. If only the decision-makers knew how many thousands of hours my mother had clocked slaving over our stove in her high heels and false eyelashes!

Still, I never saw my mother or her friends cry or complain. They'd flock to our living room and make light of the rejections. They'd swap stories of their auditions the way others swap recipes and Tupperware. "They told me I was too light." "My features are too keen, and I'm too dark." They would deflect their pain with brash, bold laughter. They would swat the insults and bad memories away with their wit, and perhaps a session of evening-gown bargain hunting.

If the motto of the Marines is *semper fidelis*—always faithful—the motto of these women is *semper* fabulous. They faced all of life's challenges and injustices with humor and irrepressible glamour.

When in my second season as a writer on *The Cosby Show* the producers Tom Werner and Marcy Carsey suggested I go and work on the show's spinoff, *A Different World*, in Los Angeles, my mother was crystal clear: I had no choice but to accept. I was being handed on a silver platter the chance to join, at its inception, a television show with one of television history's best time slots. I would receive not only a title bump, but also have the opportunity to shape this new series about life on a black college campus. I would have the opportunity to create characters modeled on the extraordinary people of color I'd known my entire life. It was the sort of break people wait years to receive. I was two years into my career, twenty-four years old, and here it was, the proverbial offer I could not refuse.

The show got off to a rocky start. Within eight weeks of beginning production, Tom Werner and Marcy Carsey scrapped the first four episodes and fired our kindly executive producer/head writer. They replaced him with a thirty-seven-year-old woman who'd been one of the only female writers on the staff of *Saturday Night Live* in its glory days, no small feat. After years of fighting to prove herself in a tough, male-dominated industry, she'd developed a brusque, sometimes cruel manner. She also held a somewhat narrow view of the black American population. In our first encounter, a "save your ass" interview, she asked me, "What is a black bitch?"

"I have no idea what you mean, what that question means," I retorted. "A bitch is a bitch."

Everyone on the show lacked soul, in her opinion.

"Just because someone isn't hoisting a boom box and speaking in the vernacular doesn't mean they're not really black," I informed her. Within five minutes she shooed me out of the room as though I were a chicken in a barnyard.

Somehow I survived her hatchet and became one of her favorite writers, though she insisted I was not a "real black girl." To that I would respond, "There are many ways to be black."

I resigned myself to being seen only in part and never fully understood. I drew strength from the lessons of my parents and of the *semper* fabulous. "You know who you are." "Lose the battle, win the war." I remembered my mother's "charm offensive" techniques for besting the enemy. I would think of my mother, Aunt Diahann Carroll, and Eartha Kitt alone in their hotel rooms around the world as young women pursuing singing careers, leaving family and the familiar behind. It was important that I succeed, because if I did, I could create parts for women like them. They had blazed trails as performers; it was my turn to blaze a trail, however small, behind the scenes.

We worked twelve- and sixteen-hour days, six and seven days a week in our headquarters, a bungalow on the

Universal Pictures lot. Our executive producer hired and fired people with such alarming speed and frequency, she should have installed a revolving door at the entrance to the writers' room. I survived by throwing out ideas incessantly and turning in scripts that didn't need much rewriting. Nonetheless, like the other writers and the cast members, I was exhausted and demoralized.

"How do we get to work? On a gurney!" This line, coined by a member of the writing team, became our gallows refrain. I resolved not to continue working under such conditions. If our head writer returned for year two, I would leave the show. Fortunately, I did not have to. By the end of the season, Marcy Carsey and Tom Werner asked this talented but tortured soul to resign.

In the course of four years, I rose from story editor to executive producer, eventually running the show with the incomparable dancer-actress-director Debbie Allen, who had just finished a long stint producing the series *Fame*. Debbie belonged to a generation of young black Broadway stars who admired my mother and felt grateful to her for opening doors. Like my mother, she refused to accept second-class citizenship and pushed to change the image of people of color.

When she first came onboard, she insisted to Mr. Cosby in the course of a breakfast meeting at his New York home that unlike *The Cosby Show*, which took place in the confines of a private home, *A Different World*, which took place on a college campus, had a duty to address racial issues head-on and to be topical. Mr. Cosby agreed, and so we tackled subjects the Huxtables could not. We did episodes on date rape, apartheid in South Africa, AIDS, the true role of the Mammy in pre–Civil War America, the little-known history of free blacks who owned slaves, the Los Angeles riots. The network did not always appreciate our forays into social relevance, to say the least.

In the case of the AIDS episode, they threatened not to pay our "license fee," that is, to cut off our financial support for the episode. We had to submit the script to several advertisers for their approval. In the end, because we cast Whoopi Goldberg in a key role and agreed to put in a parental disclaimer, they allowed us to proceed, and it became our second-highest-rated episode ever. In its aftermath, we received letters from Planned Parenthood clinics around the country informing us that the day after the episode aired, thousands had come in seeking information and testing.

We weren't performing rocket science or brain surgery, but we were proving that a television comedy could be more than an elaborate excuse to foist new brands of junk food on the American public.

I also had the satisfaction of affecting lives more closely connected to mine—I could provide gainful employment and prime-time exposure to my mother's friends. Uncle Roscoe Brown played a professor on *A Different World*. Gloria Foster played a dean. Lena Horne honored us by playing herself. I was able to write Aunt Diahann into the show as the mother of our spoiled southern belle, Whitley Gilbert. We depicted the black bourgeoisie whose existence producers and critics had denied. *The Cosby Show*, with its rainbow of blackness—the actors ranged from very dark to extremely fair—had made it possible to cast actors once shunned by white producers as "too white-looking." We took great pride and pleasure in showcasing a full range of looks and modes of being. We gave America a glimpse of the infinite variations of blackness.

For once I could do something more than listen to my mother's troubles. We cast her in *A Different World* as a sophisticated international dean. She immediately became Auntie Mame to the whole cast and to Debbie herself.

In 1991 I received a Special Recognition Award from the Friends of the Black Emmys, an organization created to recognize black actors, writers, directors, and producers and bestow upon them the statuettes they, in all likelihood, would not receive at the mainstream ceremony.

I looked out at the crowd of three hundred industry peers and told the audience, "I became a writer so that I could give my mother and all her friends jobs." I acknowledged my mother as a brilliant performer, incredible woman, exemplary wife. "You gave up a lot so that I could stand here tonight," I said. At that point, I saw tears rolling down my mother and Aunt Diahann's cheeks. They refused to weep at their own misfortunes, but this public show of gratitude delivered the coup de grace to their defenses. The *semper* fabulous sat in the romantic glow of the Versailles Room and cried.

CHAMIQUE HOLDSCLAW *is a rising star in women's professional basketball. Schooled in rough-and-tumble pickup games with boys, this native New Yorker could dunk by age twelve. After leading her high school to four consecutive state championships, she joined the dynamic Lady Vols at the University of Tennessee in 1995, helping them win three straight national championships. At six feet two, Holdsclaw was the first draft pick chosen by the Washington Mystics of the fledgling Women's National Basketball Association. The child of alcoholic parents, Chamique (pronounced Sha-mee-ka) dedicated her memoir to her most important coach, her grandmother.*

Stepping Up

I know what it must look like to outsiders, and what they must think when they see my neighborhood for the first time. When Coach Pat Summitt and her assistant, Mickie DeMoss, came from Tennessee to recruit me, Coach Vinny Cannizzaro—my high school coach—walked them from their car to my building, sure that two southern ladies in heels and suits would get a hard time in my neighborhood. Of course, he was right. They heard some whistles, some trash talk. That was just the way people were there, wary of outsiders on their turf.

Mickie says that when she got into the elevator and saw all the profanity scrawled on the walls and an empty beer can on the floor, she was horrified. *This is what Chamique has to look at every day?* she thought. She knew right away that she had to get me out of that environment. I think she and Coach Summitt thought they could save me or something. And they did give me perhaps the most amazing opportunity of my life. Playing for Tennessee was one of the greatest things that ever happened to me, and playing for Coach Summitt, hard as it was at times, made me so much better a basketball player and so much stronger a person.

But what Mickie didn't understand that day—what

almost no one understood—is that going to live in the housing project with my grandmother *is* what saved me. It was my escape. It was the place where I learned to feel safe. It was home, and still is.

I love playing basketball. In a sense, it's always been my cushion. The court was a place for me to take out my anger and frustrations without risking trouble or hurting someone else. It was my comfort zone. It was also a place where I always knew my abilities, trusted in myself.

When I was in junior high, the girls in the neighborhood used to make fun of me for spending all my time on the basketball court, playing with the boys. I was some kind of freak. Girls weren't supposed to have muscles. If you had them, you were like a man. Now, muscles are cool, muscles are the thing. I love that. I love how people accept women as athletes, women with muscles, and that's what even guys want—for women to be fit, to be strong.

Personally, I never really had body issues when I was younger. I was a gangly thing, always so thin and so tall, but I didn't dislike my body, or feel ugly or like I was some kind of freak. My feet were the only thing that could make me feel awkward or different. Now I couldn't care less, because I've grown into them, but I've had the same shoe size since I was five feet ten inches tall and in the eighth grade. It's the same shoe size Michael Jordan wears—thirteen.

When I opened the door, I didn't know what to make of Coach Summitt. She was tall and she had on a suit, and her hair was done, and her nails were done, and she had bright red lipstick. Everything about her was so put together and businesslike, except her southern drawl stuck out a little, and I didn't know whether she looked country or just fake.

I sat on the couch in our tiny living room, where my grandmother keeps my trophies and all her pictures, and my grandmother sat next to me. I was glad Mickie was there too, because Mickie was the one I'd been calling on the phone for months, building a relationship. We talked a little bit about the program and what I could expect there, but mostly we just talked.

That afternoon in our apartment, I saw right away that Coach Summitt can be intimidating. Her eyes can get to you. I could tell from the beginning that she was very well spoken and very strong. She talked about academics and graduation rates and the things she knew my grandmother thought were important. She judged right away that my grandmother and I had a special relationship and that I trusted her more than anyone, and I think she wanted to reassure my grandmother that I would be well taken care of at Tennessee, and that I would get my degree. Everything was laid out for me. They even had a study hall schedule, and could tell my grandmother how much time would be set aside for me to work on my schoolwork in an organized setting.

I liked that. I needed to know that if I left my comfort zone in Astoria and came to play at Tennessee, they were going to take care of me. I didn't want to fall through the cracks, and I knew enough about myself to know that I needed a disciplined system. I knew it would make my grandmother happy. She liked Coach Summitt, and she liked the fact that she had a 100 percent graduation rate in her program. I was going to be a Lady Vol.

A lot of people look at my relationship with Coach Summitt now and they think it was a match made in heaven. That's hilarious. Our relationship could get pretty ugly in the beginning. Coach Summitt challenged me and I just didn't understand her methods. I didn't understand what she wanted from me, and when I don't feel like I know what's expected of me, I tend to get frustrated and lose my focus. That's what happened to me freshman year.

At first, when we had conditioning at 6:00 AM, two times a week, it was tiring but fun. I liked getting to know my teammates. I thought I was ready for everything. I bought a little planner, because one thing about playing for Coach Summitt—you had to be organized. You had to keep a schedule, remember all the meetings, because you can't ever be late. She's very disciplined.

I didn't know how disciplined until we started practice. Then it felt like I could do nothing right. All day, every day, I'd hear her yelling, "Chamique! Chamique! Chamique!" It was like I was the only one out there. I'd be thinking to myself, *Dag! There are ten or eleven other people on this team. I can't be the one doing everything wrong.*

But on it went, day after day after day.

"Holdsclaw! Are you going to rebound?"

"Holdsclaw! Play some defense!"

"Chamique! Chamique! Chamique!"

The frustration inside me built and built and built until I felt I couldn't take it anymore. I felt like I couldn't talk to anyone on the team about it, because all my teammates had their own issues. I didn't know how to handle it. Here you are, you're eighteen years old, you want to be good, you want to be the best, and this lady is telling you she wants to make you the best, but all she does is yell at you. Every single day.

I'd go back to my room after practice and try to do my homework, then I'd lie in my bed, crying in the dark, trying to make sure that my roommate Kim didn't hear me. And the next day, I'd be up at Stokely, the athletic building, for individual workouts and it would be so hot, so hot up there all the time, and she'd be yelling at me again.

It was right before Christmas, and I had decided I couldn't take it anymore, when Coach Summitt finally sat down and talked to me one-on-one. We had played a game in Chicago, at DePaul. For days I had been telling Mickie that I wanted to leave, or transfer. On our flight back from Chicago, Coach Summitt called me up to sit with her on the plane. She finally gave me some positive feedback, telling me she thought I was making progress on the court. She told me she pushed me so hard because she wanted me to be the best, and she thought I had that ability. She told me she'd never push me to do something she didn't know I was capable of doing. "Just believe in me," she said. "And I'll believe in you."

Things weren't perfect after that, but they were better. We could almost always talk things out, and I think that's when Coach Summitt started to realize that what I needed was to be talked to one-on-one. Yelling at me in front of everyone was not going to get me motivated, it was only going to make me more upset. The more she learned about me, though, the more Coach Summitt knew how to push my buttons, and she pushed them again and again and again in my four years at Tennessee. Sometimes she made me furious. Sometimes she made me cry. Almost all the time, though, she made me play my best.

She pushed on every level. My grades would be decent, and she'd send me to study hall anyway. It wasn't enough for me to do OK in school. I had to excel.

"Chamique," she'd tell me, "there are certain people from whom I expect certain things. You are one of those people. I'm not going to let you sit and just do enough to get by. You have to push."

She waited, though, to see when I'd be ready to really step it up on the court in a game. Some people will say that I first really stepped up against Purdue, in early December, when I scored 27 points to lead the team. A month later, in early January, we lost a huge game to Connecticut at home—it was our first loss in our home arena in seventy games, dating back to 1991. Afterward,

Coach Summitt made all of us sit down and write our thoughts out on paper. I wrote that I had sat back and waited for the upperclassmen to step up and want the ball during the game. I wrote that I wasn't going to let that happen the next time. I wrote, "Next time, I'll step up. I want the ball."

Two weeks later, I made my big move. We were playing Vanderbilt and we were down, and I had this feeling that they couldn't guard me. I wanted the ball. I think that was the day when I really first felt this deep competitiveness inside me, a desire to succeed that canceled out any fear of failing. I just wanted to give it my all, with no fear. I scored 18 points and had 12 rebounds that night, and we ended up winning the game by 3. That was definitely a turning point for me.

Soon I was taking the ball right from the start of the game. I'd almost always be on the attack, take the first shot. That was an adjustment for Coach Summitt, who always used to tell us, "Patience, patience. Work the ball. Work it." I didn't listen. As soon as I got my hands on the ball, I wanted to attack, make things happen. I believe that when you're on a team and you are the go-to player, you need to come out with an aggressive attitude and show your opponent from the very beginning that you're going to take it to them. You have to be aggressive, but under control about it. I call it being a "quiet assassin." That opens up so many things for your teammates.

This was the attitude I took: I wanted to put people on their heels. I wanted them thinking, *Man, this kid came to play. She's all about business tonight.*

People ask me when it became "my team" at Tennessee. In high school, college, even now as a pro, I've never cared whose team it is, but there has to be somebody who is willing to take a chance. And I am willing to take a chance anytime now. Eight seconds left and you want to give me the ball? Great. I'll take the shot. You need me to make a defensive stop and guard their best player? Let me at it. Some people are scared in those types of situations and some people excel. I am just not scared. I was hesitant at the beginning of freshman year, but never again.

In the semifinals, we played Connecticut. The rivalry we had with UConn was huge, and we had been on the losing end of it lately. They'd beaten us three straight times, including in the national championship game the year before, when they went undefeated. They'd also beaten us in January, on our own court. Needless to say, we wanted blood.

The game was bitter. We kept taking the lead and they

kept fighting back—twice they recovered from double-digit deficits—and they had to get a 3-pointer at the buzzer to send it into overtime. We still won by 5. It almost felt like a miracle, because Connecticut had this twenty-game winning streak and everyone was expecting them to take us.

Georgia beat Stanford in the other semifinal, so we were going to face another team we'd lost to that season in the championship. We knew we had a tough final ahead of us. Georgia had the best player in the country, Saudia Roundtree, a senior who had been named the Naismith Player of the Year for women.

Roundtree was an incredible player, and it was going to be up to Latina Davis to guard her. I didn't envy Latina that task, but she did an amazing job. Saudia went 3-of-14 from the floor and only had 8 points. We won pretty easily, 83–65. I led our team in scoring with 16 points, and had 14 rebounds too, but I really felt like it was Latina who won the game for us. Afterward, Coach Summitt said that as a team we played nearly a perfect game, and that was something, coming from her.

It's hard to describe what it felt like to stand out there on the court after the final buzzer, with all those people cheering, and we're all hugging one another and jumping up and down and screaming. Every year in high school I'd won the championship, but it was nothing like this.

We had a party that night. What a party. We were up all night long, laughing, talking, cracking jokes. I was so excited. My grandmother was there. My little brother, Davon, was there, having a ball. And that's when I realized Coach Summitt had just taught me a lesson. There were two things she always said. One was "Tough times don't last but tough people do." The other one was "If you put in the hard work, if you pay the price, it will pay off."

After winning that championship, I felt like I could accomplish anything. It was the greatest feeling in the world.

COLIN POWELL has held high-level positions in several presidential administrations. After service in the army in Vietnam and Korea, he rose steadily through military ranks to become a four-star general. President Ronald Reagan tapped him to be national security advisor. Under President George H. W. Bush, Powell was chairman of the Joint Chiefs of Staff. In the administration of President George W. Bush, Powell was appointed secretary of state, the first African American to hold that powerful position.

Becoming a Leader

The dominant figure of my youth was a small man, five feet two inches tall. In my mind's eye, I am leaning out the window of our apartment, and I spot him coming down the street from the subway station. He wears a coat and tie, and a small fedora is perched on his head. He has a newspaper tucked under his arm. His overcoat is unbuttoned, and it flaps at his sides as he approaches with a brisk, toes-out stride. He is whistling and stops to greet the druggist, the baker, our building super, almost everybody he passes. To some kids on the block he is a faintly comical figure. Not to me. This jaunty, confident little man is Luther Powell, my father.

He emigrated from Jamaica in his early twenties, seventeen years before I was born. He left his family and some sort of menial job in a store to emigrate. No doubt he came to this country for the reason that propelled millions before him, to become something more than he had been and to give his children a better start than he had known. He literally came to America on a banana boat, a United Fruit Company steamer that docked in Philadelphia.

My mother came from a slightly more elevated social

station in Jamaica. She had a high school education, which my father lacked. When I picture Mom, she is wearing an apron, bustling around our apartment, always in motion, cooking, washing, ironing, sewing, after working all day downtown in the garment district as a seamstress, sewing buttons and trim on clothing.

He was the eternal optimist, my mother the perennial worrier. That never changed, no matter how much our fortunes did.

I grew up largely at 952 Kelly Street in the Hunts Point section of the South Bronx, where my family had moved in 1943, when I was six. In those days Hunts Point was heavily Jewish, mixed with Irish, Polish, Italian, black, and Hispanic families. The block of Kelly Street next to ours was slightly curved, and the neighborhood had been known for years as "Banana Kelly." We lived in tenements. Outsiders often have a sense of New York as big, overwhelming, impersonal, anonymous. Actually, even now it's a collection of neighborhoods where everybody knows everybody's business, the same as in a small town. Banana Kelly was like that.

When I was nine, catastrophe struck the Powell family. As a student at P.S. 39, I passed from the third to the fourth grade, but into the bottom form, called "Four Up," a euphemism meaning the kid is a little slow. This was the sort of secret to be whispered with shaking heads in our family circle. Education was the escape hatch, the way up and out for West Indians. My sister was already an excellent student, destined for college. And here I was, having difficulty in the fourth grade. I lacked drive, not ability. I was a happy-go-lucky kid, amenable, amiable, and aimless.

As a boy, I took piano lessons; but the lessons did not take with me, and they soon ended. I gave up the flute too. Apparently, I would not be a jock or a musician. Still, I was a contented kid, growing up in the warmth and security of the concentric circles my family formed. Family members looked out for, prodded, and propped up each other.

At family gatherings, talk would invariably turn to "goin' home." No matter how many years my aunts and uncles had been in America, when they said home, they meant Jamaica. They would slip into nostalgia, all but my godfather, Uncle Shirley, a dining-car waiter on the Pennsylvania Railroad. Uncle Shirley was Jamaican, too, but in their eyes, he had gone "American," even shedding much of his West Indian accent after riding the rails for so many years with native-born blacks. "Goin' home?" Uncle Shirley would say. "You sit around talking about 'home.' You forget why we left? Ain't been home in twenty years, and I ain't never going home." At which point the kids would laugh uproariously, delighted to see Uncle Shirley provoked.

Our family was a matriarchy. I loved my uncles—they were the sauce, the fun, and they provided the occasional rascal. But most were weaker personalities than their wives. The women set the standards, whipped the kids into shape, and pushed them ahead. The exception was my father. Luther Powell, maybe small, maybe unimposing in appearance, maybe somewhat comical, was nevertheless the ringmaster of this family circle.

His take-charge manner was reassuring. Luther Powell never let his race or station affect his sense of self. West Indians like him had come to this country with nothing. Every morning they got on that subway, worked like dogs all day, got home at eight o'clock at night, supported their families, and educated their children. If they could do that, how dare anyone think they were less than anybody's equal? That was Pop's attitude.

Of course, there was always the dream that it might not

have to be earned by the sweat of your brow, that one day Dame Fortune might step in.

The Bronx can be a cold harsh place in February, and it was frigid the day I set out for college. After two bus rides, I was finally deposited, shivering, in Harlem. I got out and craned my neck like a bumpkin in from the sticks, gazing at handsome brownstones and apartment houses. This was the best of Harlem, where blacks with educations and good jobs lived, the Gold Coast.

I stopped at the corner of Convent and 141st and looked into the campus of the City College of New York. I was about to enter a college established in the previous century "to provide higher education for the children of the working class." Ever since then, New York's poorest and brightest have seized that opportunity. As I took in the grand Gothic structures, a C-average student, I felt overwhelmed.

During my first semester at CCNY, something had caught my eye—young guys on campus in uniform. CCNY was a hotbed of liberalism, radicalism, even some leftover communism from the 1930s; it was not a place where you would expect much of a military presence. When I returned to school in the fall, I enrolled in ROTC

[Reserve Officers' Training Corps]. I was not alone. CCNY had the largest voluntary ROTC contingent in America, fifteen hundred cadets at the height of the Korean War.

There came a day when I stood in line in the drill hall to be issued olive-drab pants and jacket, brown shirt, brown tie, brown shoes, a belt with a brass buckle, and an overseas cap. As soon as I got home, I put the uniform on and looked in the mirror. I liked what I saw. At this point, not a single Kelly Street friend of mine was going to college. I was seventeen. I felt cut off and lonely. The uniform gave me a sense of belonging, and something I had never experienced all the while I was growing up; I felt distinctive.

My experience in high school, on basketball and track teams, and briefly in Boy Scouting had never produced a sense of belonging. The Pershing Rifles did. For the first time in my life I was a member of a brotherhood.

The discipline, the structure, the camaraderie, the sense of belonging were what I craved. I became a leader almost immediately. I found a selflessness within our ranks that reminded me of the caring atmosphere within my family. Race, color, background, income meant nothing. The PRs would go to the limit for each other and for the group. If this was what soldiering was all about, then maybe I wanted to be a soldier.

I returned to college commuting from Kelly Street. I did not have to be an urbanologist to see that the old neighborhood was deteriorating. The decline was just the latest chapter in the oldest story in New York, people moving up and out as their fortunes improved and poorer people moving in to take their places. One day, I came home from CCNY to find that a kid I knew had been found in a hallway, dead of a heroin overdose. He would not be the last.

The secret dream of tenement dwellers had always been to own their own home. My father also dreamed about numbers. Then, one Saturday night, my father dreamed a number, and the next morning at St. Margaret's Church the same number appeared on the hymn board. This, surely, was God taking Luther Powell by the hand. I still remember the atmosphere of joy, disbelief, and anxiety when the numbers runner delivered the brown paper bags to our house, $10,000 in tens and twenties, more than three years' pay. And that was how the Powells managed to buy 183-68 Elmira Avenue, in the community of Hollis in the borough of Queens.

I was no great shakes as a scholar. I have joked over the years that the CCNY faculty handed me a diploma, uttering a sigh of relief, and were happy to pass me along to the military. Yet, even this C-average student emerged from CCNY prepared to write, think, and communicate effectively and equipped to compete against students from colleges that I could never have dreamed of attending. I am, consequently, a champion of public secondary and higher education. I will speak out for them and support them for as long as I have the good sense to remember where I came from.

I can remember the moment I had my first doubt about the career I had chosen. It happened in the mountains of northern Georgia as I hurtled along a cable at a height of one hundred feet, seconds from being smashed against a large tree. This exercise was called the Slide for Life, and the army was making me perform it to see if I was scared. I was.

The slide also tested our willingness to obey what seemed like suicidal orders. The cable had been strung across a river, attached to trees at either end, starting high, then sloping steeply. At my turn I grabbed a hook attached to a pulley that ran along the cable. The challenge was to ride the cable and not let go until the instructor on the other bank yelled, "Drop!" Suddenly I was careening down the wire at terrifying speed, the tree on the other side, looking bigger and bigger, rushing up to meet me. At what seemed the last possible second, he yelled, and I plunged into the water a dozen feet from the tree. It was one of the most frightening experiences of my life.

The Slide for Life was one of the joys cooked up for us during the two months at Ranger school that followed eight weeks of basic infantry training at Fort Benning, Georgia. By the time the basic course ended, the meaning of "Follow Me" had been hammered home. The infantry officer was to go into battle up front, demonstrating courage, determination, strength, proficiency, and selfless sacrifice. We were to march into hell, if necessary, to accomplish the mission. At the same time, we were taught to fulfill this responsibility while trying to keep ourselves and our men from being killed.

We were taught at Fort Benning, however, that American soldiers must know the reason for their sacrifices. If the duty of the soldier is to risk his life, the responsibility of his leaders is not to spend that life in vain. When I rose to a position where I had to recommend where to risk American lives, I never forgot that principle.

After Ranger school, I reported for airborne training. Rappelling off cliffs, sliding for life, and jumping out of airplanes answered a question that I think everyone secretly asks. Do I have physical courage? I dreaded doing these things. If I never have to parachute again, that will be fine with me, yet there was never any doubt in my mind that I could do what had to be done. These experiences are rites of passage. Physical danger that people face and master together bonds them in some mystical way. And conquering one's deepest fears is exhilarating.

DEXTER SCOTT KING *was only seven years old when his father, Rev. Dr. Martin Luther King, Jr., was assassinated in 1968. Growing up, he was expected to follow in his father's footsteps as a civil rights leader. Instead, he tried to find his own way, delving into such fields as police work and music and film production. Restless, conflicted, and unfulfilled, it was only as a grown man that he could push past the web of doubts surrounding his father's murder. Opening a prison door led to a confrontation—with truth and with himself—that he had been waiting for all his life.*

My Father's Son

Daddy was not just charismatic away from home. His personal magnetism had nothing to do with the Civil Rights Movement on the level I'm talking about. I'd watch him when he wasn't looking, in different states of activity or repose. He insisted we have family time to discuss what was going on, and why he had to be away.

Him sitting at the dining room table with us was a good time for conversation. I can still see him walking down the hallway at home in his slippers. He had a burgundy-colored satin-like robe he always wore to breakfast. Whenever he wore his robe, I was happy, because it meant he wasn't going anywhere for a while. Many times he felt like a playmate, like somebody who was Dad in terms of compassion and sensitivity, but was not so removed, because he enjoyed playing too, and could relate to a child's problems.

When he'd come back from a trip, we'd hide from him, trembling with excitement; he'd find us, have us jump off the refrigerator into his arms. He called it the Kissing Game. We'd jump into his arms, take our turns; there were four of us, he divided his time equally—what little he had left. He tried his best. More than just having a spot on his face to kiss, he had an intimate spot in his heart for everybody; we felt it, it made us feel special. He knew how to relate on our level. He was a universal communicator, even to his children, and he knew how to embrace you in a way where you felt part of some greater plan.

Most people might think, because of the way he was projected as such a serious person, that he was always so, but sometimes he was the opposite of that, or the balance of that; he needed an outlet, a way to break the tension. He sought refuge in his children, his family. We had no idea of the momentous nature of Daddy's work. He and his colleagues were about ending the system of segregation in American life, no small or simple matter.

My mother would get frustrated because I seemed to have a great need to know why. I was the type that came across like I was questioning authority; but I had a need to explore and see how things worked. I think Mother even took it as me being defiant. But I didn't feel defiant. She didn't have much tolerance for foolishness either way. She'd spank us—"whip" us, as they call it in the country. My father wouldn't. He didn't spank us. He would deal more on a mental level, try to get us to understand why things were.

One day my brother, Martin, my cousin, Isaac, and I came across a treasure trove. Plastic toy guns! Immediately we were having a ball, playing army, playing war, playing gangsters, cops and robbers, the Untouchables, cowboys and Indians. We were going "bang! bang!" feigning death throes, the things boys do when they play with guns. Daddy must have been watching from a window. He came out, sat down heavily, gathered us at his knee.

The indoctrination of children who are being exposed to violent instruments of war—he didn't want to see it happen to his sons, his nephews, or anybody, but it was hard if not impossible to stop it, even within the borders of his own home. My father extended his palm and asked us for the guns.

"The guns these toys represent have one use. They're used only to kill or maim people. If you saw what they did to people, you'd be sad. Suppose somebody shot somebody you loved?"

I looked at him as if to say, No, that could never be, thinking as a child that "bang-bang" meant you were "dead," but you could get up and argue about whether you were "dead" or not.

"You don't want another human being's death on your conscience," my father said. "You want to have life. I'd rather see you boys play sports like football than play with guns. I'd rather you play a musical instrument, debate, or even fight . . . but not with these."

He talked with us for a while longer. The way he spoke was so effective that at the end of it he actually had us destroy those plastic guns. We put them in a metal trash can and burned them, melted them down. I didn't fully understand it then. But I was moved by what my father had said.

The last Christmas we all shared was in 1967. At the time, we didn't know it was the last Christmas we'd all share. It was just another great Christmas. Mother bought my father and me identical bicycles. Mine was just a junior version of his. Same brand, same color, same style. A purple metallic, sparkly color that transfixed me; a new model.

We rode our bikes on the streets of Vine City, past shotgun houses, Egan Homes, Magnolia Ballroom, Flavor Palace, Pascal's, the Ollie Street Y, Washington Park—our world. My father had insisted that we be in an environment where we would be with the people, not be on a mountain talking down to the valley, but in the valley, and perhaps go up the mountain together one day, in a perfect world.

The couple of months after Daddy's and my birthdays

in January of 1968 felt ominous. Martin, Yolanda, and myself asked Daddy not to go to Memphis. The three of us felt it. Something bad was going to happen. He knew it better than we did. How we picked up on it, I don't know. It was a frustrating period for all of us because we felt we had no control.

We were watching television. That's how I learned. TV told me. The special bulletin came on, and an unforgettable voice said, "Dr. Martin Luther King Jr. has been shot in Memphis at 6:01 PM."

Martin and I looked at each other. We said nothing. We both jumped up and ran back into our parents' bedroom.

Mother sat on their bed, ankles crossed, fingers of her free hand and the phone receiver at her mouth. "Mother? Mommy? Mama? You hear that? What do they mean?"

Mother held up a finger, telling us to be patient, quiet, to wait; she was being briefed. We waited for her to get off the phone—and dreaded her getting off.

She kept saying, "I understand." I'll never forget those words, how I couldn't understand why she would keep repeating them. Pain filled Mother's face. She encircled us boys in her arms and drew in a deep breath, as if about to dive underwater.

"Your father—there's been an accident." From then on our mother was stoic. She made you feel she was in control.

"Mommy, when is Daddy coming home?" I kept repeating.

"I'm going to Memphis to see Daddy, Dexter. When I get there I'll call and let you know."

"OK."

Then they left for the airport. Sooner than expected, she would come back. She arrived at the airport and was informed there was no reason to rush. Her husband, our father, was dead.

Hope went out of many lives. We were not alone in that, and never would be alone in it from then on. Wherever America went, particularly black America, we'd go careening with it.

Funeral over, repast done, visitors gone home. For the survivors, the river of life goes on, but the comforting course it takes has been unalterably diverted. Extended family leaves. You're there alone. Just your mother, sisters, brother, and conscience.

Some people are fine doing the routine, following a tradition. Such was not the case for me. I think of Bernice and Yolanda and Martin, and each, in his or her own way, was fine and good following traditional steps. I was not. I wanted to find a connection to something inspirational. I looked for it in a book, in a classroom, but didn't find it there.

I did have a need, as my father did, to be understood and gain understanding. I wanted—needed—to contribute in life. Like most young men, I had not found my mission and I didn't have the same interests Daddy had. By the time he was twenty-five he was ready to pastor; by the time he was twenty-six, political machinations or not, back door or not, his idea or not, he was the leader of the Montgomery bus boycott. I needed space to experiment and figure out who I, Dexter, wanted to be. But this need seemed to always put me at odds with society, and well-intentioned people, who wanted me to be what they wanted: the second coming of a King.

I went to work in 1982 for the Atlanta Police Department. I started out as a community service officer, poised to become a police recruit, then changed to corrections officer, all under the umbrella of the Department of Public Service.

The police investigator who was doing my background

check seemed befuddled—"You're Martin Luther King's son?" He didn't get it. A lot of other people had that look on their faces, too. "What's the motivation here—what's your story, King boy, like you think you can just come in here and get a job here because of who you are?"

But it was good exposure. By exploring a career in law enforcement, I'd decided to act on my own curiosities for a change. It had a cost. I'd come by the King Center on Auburn Avenue after work, still in uniform, sidearm on, to see Mother. Some people would say, "How can you come in here, in this building, with a weapon?" I thought about the plastic toy guns, and Daddy.

For whatever reason, I was able to separate that this was a job; it didn't make me not my father's son. That's always been a subconscious consideration of each of my adult acts. I never had to use my sidearm. I was trained to do it, and I didn't see it as diametrically opposed to nonviolence, as long as the greater good prevailed.

I was there because I wanted to learn; you can't affect a thing unless you know it, how it works. You have to get in there and see it. I never want to seem like a guy talking about things from afar, so I'd worked hard and learned a lot. I'd been there and done that, I know security issues, the criminal justice system from a practical level. I got what I needed out of it.

A lot of what I needed came from the head of the bureau, who was both a mentor and a father figure. J. D. Hudson was a stern man. Not a big man, but a presence—his voice, his way, and his manner. Hudson was no-nonsense. So I think he was disappointed when I told him I felt I had to muster out, yet I think he also knew there were other things for me to do. I talked to him about how I felt traumatized by losing my father, and how maybe that was one reason I wanted to spend some time on the force. But now it was time to move on.

J. D. Hudson sighed and said, "Listen here. You don't need to be feeling sorry for yourself. You know how many other people lost their fathers, just on April 4, 1968? Do you want me to go through a census records check, just so you can see how many died that day, and how?"

I squirmed in my chair. "No. No, sir." I'd never thought of it that way before.

Hudson said, "You come from better timber than that. Some people don't even know their father. You can't use your father being killed, or not being here for you, every time you have a crisis, as some kind of an excuse."

He said I was fortunate to have had not only a great father, but a great mother. And I knew that. He said, "You
be thankful for what you got, and what you had." I'd heard
similar comments, but never as strongly and logically
worded and never from a man I respected so much. I
cherished him and that experience.

Ever since I stood on that balcony where Daddy stood and
was killed, I knew eventually I'd ask, "Why?" and "How?"
We needed to confront the issue of the assassination, look
at it squarely. You can put seeking the truth off to one
side. But then there comes a time when you just can't keep
hiding from it anymore, when it's affecting your life so
profoundly, so deeply, it no longer can be ignored except
at the peril of your own life, health, sanity. Most people
view my father's assassination as a world event, another
moment of collective horror, as it surely was. But as time
has passed, they seem to have forgotten that it was equally
a very personal event; that it was the defining tragedy in
the lives of my mother, my siblings, and me. We needed
closure to find real peace.

James Earl Ray, the convicted assassin of Rev. Martin
Luther King Jr. was running out of time. His liver was

quitting. But before the end, Ray found some comfort. From the King family itself.

"I just want to ask for the record—did you kill my father?" I asked.

"No," claimed the sixty-nine-year-old convict.

When I met with Ray, this was the sense I got: he was a petty criminal who had done stupid things. He didn't have much common sense and said as much. "Look, I ain't gonna tell you I'm totally innocent here. I did mess up and make mistakes. But I did not shoot Dr. King."

I felt the guy got a bum rap. I felt he was a patsy.

We were in collective shock in 1968 when James Earl Ray was shot through the legal system as if greased. "Try to move on," I remember people saying. As if. As time went on, deep down inside, all the adults in my family felt there was more to it. I, me, Dexter, ended up as point man for all those years of muffled questions and suppressed doubts. My family looked to me now. The feeling was, no matter who is involved, what can you do? You felt helpless to do anything else but think about it, roll it over in your mind, try and figure it out.

Even if Ray did it, did he do it alone? The force of will behind this murder—did he possess that? Was he that brave, that resourceful, to escape under the noses of law enforcement without any help? Was he competent enough to make that shot? I believe whoever killed Daddy was aided and abetted. It was not a one-man deal. We didn't pursue a new trial for any other reason than to get the truth on the permanent record, so we could feel like we'd done everything we could've done. We owed Daddy that.

Freedom never comes easy. Neither does life; maybe that's part of my contribution. Maybe to show how easy it isn't, is my contribution. I don't know. I've learned that not knowing is permissible—it carries no shame. Part of a journey is struggle, failure. You still must give yourself permission to live. Would he approve? Would he disapprove? I let it go. I didn't follow tradition, but it wasn't because I didn't want to be about my father's business. It was part of a greater plan. It's not sad. It's life.

ANTWONE FISHER *works in Hollywood as a screenwriter and producer. His first produced screenplay tells the dramatic and often heart-wrenching story of his own life. Born in prison to a single mother, he spent the next eighteen years living in a succession of miserable environments: an orphanage, several foster homes, a reform school for boys, a homeless shelter, and, finally, on the streets of Cleveland. The 2002 movie* Antwone Fisher, *directed by Denzel Washington, was based on Fisher's memoir,* Finding Fish.

Leaving the Twilight Zone

The first thing you notice when you're homeless is how long the nights are. You don't really sleep, especially in the beginning, because you wake up every fifteen minutes worried someone will come upon you. Your imagination runs wild with what terrible things would happen if you fell asleep and let that happen.

The world at night when you're without shelter feels like the Twilight Zone, another dimension, another planet, where the normal laws of time and space don't apply. When the sun comes up, you're so happy knowing that soon people are going to be out and you'll be back in the world again, on terra firma, although you're tired and worried about how fast night comes again.

Before you know it, you're seeing the shops close down, lights diminishing down streets, cars becoming fewer and fewer; on residential blocks you enviously watch working mothers and fathers pulling into driveways, arriving home to their families; and you stand outside talking to them in your head, saying, *Don't go inside, not yet, stay out a little longer!*

Your hearing changes as the general noise of the worka- day world goes silent and other sounds become more pronounced. A car engine sputtering. Tires squealing around turns. Even sounds that are far away: distant trains, speeding cars, gunshots, police and ambulance sirens.

Soon you get used to the night smells. You may notice that broken glass has its own smell. The various smells of wine bottles mixed with the other varieties of liquor and beer are distinct, too. These smells compete with the smells of rats, wet plaster, and rotting wood, the smell of a hollow place. And you can hardly avoid the recurring smell of human feces and urine.

Night holds a separate world that can be far more brutal than sleeping in abandoned storefronts and alleyways and on park benches. It is the criminal business world where hardened humans prey upon the weaknesses and misfortunes of others, a world populated by men and women, many of them young, who lost their way a long time ago. The night is host to this soulless world where parents loan their children to deviants for drugs or whatever else satisfies their empty hearts. This is a world you may never want to know, but it's a world that exists; it exists everywhere and probably has always existed.

When you're homeless and you're a kid, that world is waiting for you and is always on the lookout for new recruits. If you're a girl, God have mercy on you. If you're a boy, God have mercy on you, too. You don't need an invitation to come in, doesn't matter what you look like: fat, small, black, white, tall, Chinese . . . if you can breathe, if you're young and homeless, you're drafted.

In my opinion, homelessness is preferable to being sucked into the machinery of the night. As a matter of fact, I think everyone should experience being homeless and going without. You get a different perspective on everything and a different appreciation for everything. You come to understand that you can be living in a house and still be homeless, as I was in the foster home and in the institutions where I later went to live.

You learn what it feels like to be invisible to all those carefree or self-preoccupied people walking by you, maybe sidestepping the spot where you stand in order not to see you, or driving obliviously by you. Depending on your state of mind, you might prefer being invisible—as I did. If you've never been on the street, perhaps you may not see its world and all its inhabitants. But once you've been there yourself, you develop an extraterrestrial vision, and you see everyone who lives there. You retain your otherworldly eyes, even after you leave, and no matter how your own circumstances improve, you will continue to see the world that lies in shadows just beyond the gates; and you understand how easy it is to be pushed back out.

With the criminal underworld so ready to prey on unprotected minors, offering money and housing in return for work, the sight of a homeless seventeen-year-old may not be so common. Even the wino who slept for a while in the same storefront I did was sure I was a runaway. He kept trying to convince me to go back, no matter how bad it was at home. It took me a long time to convince him that I didn't have that option.

Three days before Christmas I spent the night in an alley downtown, not alone; in fact, there were a lot of people huddling in blankets, vying for space. That was a piercing cold I'd never felt before, with the icy winds blowing off the lake and funneled by the tall buildings like a supersonic death-destroying weapon.

In that mind-and-body-numbing state the idea of the military made some sense. It couldn't be any worse than this. I had passed by this recruiting office often but this was the first time I'd noticed this poster that lured me inside. It directed me to the attention of two recruiting officers who may have assumed correctly from my disheveled, frozen appearance that I was homeless.

It was an old-fashioned movie-style poster with the word *Heritage* printed in large ornate letters at the top. In the background was a wooden sailing ship, and in the foreground was a sailor, dressed in a crackerjack uniform, holding the hand of a boy as the two gazed off into the distance together—toward adventure, fun, and glamour. And at the bottom, in bold, inviting type was the phrase that really got me: *Join the Navy, See the World.*

From the first night that I arrived at boot camp in Great Lakes, Illinois, two nights before Christmas, I've had people barking orders at me, determined to drive out all traces of civilian blood from my body. It began the instant we stepped off the bus into what felt like arctic cold and met up with the rest of our company. Out of the dark came a chorus of orders to march. Eighty of us—black, white, Asian, Hispanic, from many walks of life, all young men—proceeded to march, each in a different timing, everybody bumping into one another, stepping on each other's heels. Total havoc.

Our days were exhausting, filled with instruction as basic as how to properly press and fold every article of clothing that we wore, down to our briefs, to detailed academic courses, to pounding physical training. Every day we were given inspections and tests. If you failed any of the inspections, if one T-shirt wasn't folded to absolute perfection, you were given MTU—extra military training that required running through an obstacle course set up in a massive drill hall while you held a rifle aloft over your head. Any kind of mild infraction of rules, including falling asleep at any time during the day, would result in MTU. Like everyone, I feared and dreaded MTU. But not once did that happen.

Failing any of our weekly tests resulted in something far worse than MTU—being sent back a week. Here the navy really had me scared. Eventually, if you were sent back enough times, you were deemed unqualified to serve and given a discharge.

Out of eighty recruits in my company, twenty or so were eventually sent back or discharged. Whenever any of them failed a test, their names were called afterward and they were told to wait outside. We never saw them again. Through every week, through every test, I listened with a clench in my gut, sure that the next name asked to wait outside was going to be mine. It never was. I passed every test.

Up until now, with the exception of Mrs. Profit's class from fourth through sixth grade and my popular period in junior high, I'd been below average. But boot camp gave me a new self-image. I found out that I was average, academically and athletically. In some instances, I was even above average, especially when it came to cleaning and organization, as well as adhering to rules and regulations. If my upbringing in institutions had prepared me for anything, it was definitely those aspects of the navy.

I may have also had an easier time in the way that boot camp sought to eliminate our individuality. After all, my individuality had never been allowed to flourish before. And I didn't suffer like most of the other homesick recruits who existed for daily letters from home and girlfriends.

Not that there weren't days when I thought I couldn't do it anymore. But when faced with quitting, as a few in my company did, I knew that wasn't an option for me. If I quit, I'd be right back on the street, homeless again. For now, grueling as it was, boot camp was my home, the best place for me.

In San Diego, the U.S.S. *Schenectady* LST 1185, a troop landing ship that could physically pull up onto the beach and open its bow to deploy marine tanks, was in the midst of an overhaul. After our overhaul, the *Schenectady* was elected to assist in qualifying marine helicopter pilots to land on a ship in motion. Initially my job on that relatively small deck landing area was as one of four chockers who stood in pairs to either side of the man whose job it was to give hand signals to the incoming helicopters. Once the helicopter landed, we ran together, two to a side, and secured the helicopter's wheels to the ship with chains and blocks, also known as chocks.

After three days of chocking, Chief Elmer Fudd decides I'm ready for the most important job on the flight deck— guiding the helicopter into landing. After some training, here I am in the brisk ocean spray coming off the high seas, with a battalion of Hueys heading toward the ship, getting the cursing of a lifetime because the chief thinks I'm ready and I know I'm not.

In theory, I have it down—waving the pilot toward me with one hand, waving two hands to the side for when to stay in position, then waving toward me again. But in practice, I can just see myself freezing up and forgetting the proper signals and sending the Huey and its pilot crashing into one of the ship's tall stacks, killing and maiming everyone.

"You don't understand!" I argue with the chief. *You*

don't know me, I want to say, *how can you put everybody's lives in my hands?*

As I back away from him, Elmer Fudd takes off his helmet—his brain bucket, he calls it—and throws it at me, hitting me in the chest. "You hear me? Get over there and do what I tell you to do!"

As the Huey gets closer still, bigger still, louder still, I look up to see the shadowed face of the pilot trained on me. With his head gear, his features are hidden in a dark, ominous mask, but I can tell that he is watching me and waiting for my direction. The chief and everyone on deck are watching and waiting. And then I'm doing it, I'm bringing him in, convinced still that it's too much responsibility for me, that I'll send him off course, because my luck is not for it to work out, my luck is for this to be the worst day of my life. I freeze again and the chief explodes.

A jolt of electricity pulses through me as my arms move, correctly, decisively, and I give the signal, the right signal, and the helicopter lands, bounces a little, and stays. Just like that. I signal for the chockers to secure the Huey to the deck and they do.

The chief walks over to me and nods his head. "See? You can do it. Now let's see you do it again."

For the next hour, I guide a dozen Hueys to safe landings and takeoffs. The more I do it, the more confident I am. And when the chief tells me it's somebody else's turn, I don't want to stop. I can't wait until the next time I can do this job and experience this unforgettable feeling of power, purpose, and importance that springs from the realization that everybody was depending on me and I didn't let them down.

In the book of my new life, I am not only able to be responsible for myself, but I can be responsible for others— for their lives. In this one day on the deck of the U.S.S. *Schenectady*, from the goading-on of a chief boatswain who reminds me of Elmer Fudd, I meet and greet my powerful self, thus leaving childhood and being born a man.

LYNNE DUKE *is a newspaper journalist. From 1995 to 1999 she worked as the Johannesburg bureau chief for the* Washington Post. *From her base in South Africa she traveled widely, covering the most important social and political events taking place in the continent south of the equator. Duke brought to her adventurous profession the special perspectives of being an African American and a woman. While her experiences in Africa left her both exhilarated and discouraged, she remains cautiously optimistic about the future. Duke still sees hope for its people, though many continue to live uneasily between famine, fear, and freedom.*

Dispatch from Africa

I hated it when the lights went out. I still had a dispatch to write, for Washington was awaiting my daily file. But there I sat, foiled again, fumbling for my flashlight and candles as the whole of Kinshasa, capital of the Democratic Republic of Congo, was reduced to the darkness of a village. It was August 1998, in the midst of yet another Congo war, and those damned rebels had done it again. They'd seized the country's main hydroelectric plant and taunted Kinshasa, and me, with another nightly blackout.

I fumed to myself as I lit a candle and welcomed the eerie glow it cast over my room. I lodged up on the fourteenth floor of the Hotel Intercontinental, and down below, as far as the eye could see across the sprawling metropolis, cooking fires and candlelight speckled the darkness like stars fallen to the ground. My people, African people, were suffering again. And my people, African people, were the cause. This was getting pathetic.

I pored through my notepads, jam-packed with days of scribbled shorthand, and raced against time as I wrote. I could only hope my laptop battery would outlast the night's power outage; only hope I'd make it through another Washington deadline. Night after night, my dispatches grew more ominous. The rebel juggernaut pressed closer to the capital. Food shortages deepened. Ethnic cleansing swept through the streets. Massacres unfolded all around the country. President Laurent Kabila's regime girded for a fight that his splintered army could not win. The United States, France, Belgium, and Britain evacuated their nationals but had no intention of rescuing Kinshasa itself. So African leaders stepped into the void, assembling a response of their own to the bloodbath that many feared would consume the city's 5 million people.

That was my fear too. The days ahead would be dangerous. I didn't know how I'd make it through. I had a fever and needed sleep. I needed a hot bath in clean water that wouldn't plant strange bacteria on my skin. Sick with the bends from the hotel's lovely display of a faintly rancid buffet, I craved fresh food. And what I wouldn't give for a doctor to do something about the infected boil on my face. It bulged from my cheek like a third eye. It assaulted my vanity each time I looked in the mirror, and disgusted my colleagues as they watched the boil grow.

Strangely, it reminded me of my mother back in Los Angeles. If she could see me now, I laughed to myself.

Mom thought mine such a glamorous profession and regaled friends and relatives with tales of my travels. But I am certain she never imagined that a foreign correspondent for the famed *Washington Post* could look as worn and diseased as I'd become—on the road, in Africa, at war.

There was no way out. The borders were closed. And even if I could have gone, I'd have opted to stay. I had a job to do, a mission to fulfill. A certain degree of misguided heroism kept me going, as if Congo needed me to be there to write its latest chapter. It was a delusion, I know. But I'd placed myself fully inside Africa's unfolding story.

Change and upheaval roared through central and southern Africa in the 1990s, and that was my territory. Some of it was inspiring. After decades of white-minority rule called apartheid, South Africa had turned to democracy under President Nelson Mandela in 1994—a change that freed southern Africa as a whole and opened the prospect of South African–led peace and development. But farther north, the central African region reeled from the 1994 genocide in Rwanda that left some eight hundred thousand people slaughtered. Rwanda's blood spilled throughout the region and was the spark that ignited two wars next door, in Congo.

I'd written through the first war, the one in 1997. That conflict unseated Mobutu Sese Seko, the infamously grandiose and corrupt dictator when the country was called Zaire. And now, only fifteen months later, Mobutu's disastrous successor, Laurent Désiré Kabila, seemed certain to meet the same fate. Kinshasa, again, was the epicenter of events shaping my notions of Africa.

During the day, free of the nighttime curfews and power outages, it felt strange to venture through a suddenly silent city. Kinshasa, normally, is a place of high-decibel noise—loud conversation, loud music, rumba and *ndombolo*; loud traffic. You could hear old cars banging down the road, parts scraping against each other, bouncing along crumbled, potholed streets choked with exhaust fumes, honking horns, and shouting people. But all that was gone. No sashaying women, their hips draped in garishly gorgeous cloth; no market women with necks taut from the loads they bore on their heads. Even the ragtag, malnourished children who hawked soap, cigarettes, and facial tissues on every corner were scarce.

Instead, angry troops were on the prowl, including those twitchy teens with guns, the child soldiers. I'd become all too familiar with the barrel of the AK-47, having had so many pointed in my car window by these power-mad juveniles. Nationalism had exploded. Ethnic chauvinism became deadly. Kabila's brutish regime stoked it. The army rounded up all Tutsis—or any tall person with angular features that fit the ethnic Tutsi stereotype—and detained, tortured, even killed them, on suspicion of complicity with the rebel force spearheaded by Rwanda and its Tutsi-led military. As rebels infiltrated the city, some civilians took matters into their own hands. On the streets, they burned suspected insurgents to death, no matter their ethnic background.

For thirty days, I clenched my teeth. Dodging soldiers and roadblocks, I moved through the city interviewing local people as well as foreign diplomats. I worked the cell phone as I drove around with Tom Tshibangu, my translator and tireless assistant, and Pierre Mabele, the driver and strategist of Kinshasa's mean streets. Both had become true friends in a pinch.

The war roaring toward the city had pumped me with adrenaline. I attacked it, journalistically, like an obsession. Seeing Congo face yet another setback made me passionately angry, for I knew that Congo was on its own. No matter how bad things got, I feared there'd be no rescue, no intervention to save the thousands of African lives being lost. The West would watch and warn combatants to retreat, but nothing more. *So, fine,* I thought. With my dispatches, read in Washington but also around the world, I could at least rub people's faces in it day after day after day.

This sounds less than objective, I know. I was there to observe and tell the story, not to get emotionally caught up in it. But in the best of times, I am a true believer that journalism should comfort the afflicted. And in these, the worst of times, my sensibilities could not withstand the daily onslaught of fear and death, of sources and friends living under the gun. I felt swept up in a storm far larger than journalism.

When mortar blasts rocked me awake one morning toward month's end, I was actually glad. Whoever was bombing whom, I was willing to bet the endgame had arrived. Angola, Zimbabwe, and Namibia, Kabila's allies, had been planning for some days to help save the capital, and as I sat straight up in bed that morning, I hoped that was what they were doing. Luckily, I slept fully clothed. It took only a couple of minutes to slide into my shoes, do some quick ablutions, and grab my gear before running down the stairwell (yes, fourteen flights) to find out what was going on.

To my relief, I learned from diplomats around the city that the allies were fighting rebels out in the city's crowded eastern neighborhoods, toward the airport. From the city center, we could hear the fighting that raged for three days, though journalists couldn't get anywhere near it. But we lined our balconies one night and witnessed a terrifying sight. Near the fringes of the blacked-out city, the sky exploded. I hated the thought of it, but this was war.

Leaving the Intercon, a pack of us foreign correspondents, about a dozen all told, headed to the Congo River. The airport remained closed, so a river ferry was our only way out. It would take us to Brazzaville, capital of the Congo Republic, and from there we could fly out on a British or French military transport.

We weren't the only ones trying to flee. Crowds of local people with their bags and children in tow milled about near the rotting docks and jetties. Apparently, ordinary people wouldn't be allowed to board our ferry. The people watched us. Their gaze seemed resentful, or maybe my guilt made it look that way. I would be getting out. They would stay. They would have to endure more of a city with no electricity, no water, dwindling food supplies, and legions of trigger-happy teens.

An armed gang of immigration officials, soldiers, and plainclothes security men swarmed among us. They shoved and shouted angrily. They snatched up our luggage for thorough searches, as if we foreigners surely had some incriminating possessions. Any papers or documents would only bring interrogation, or worse, so I'd hidden mine in my pants and in my suitcase lining. Sweat dripped down my chest. My boil had begun to ooze. My nerves seemed about to snap. But soon I'd be on my way. As we lined up to board, the crowd of locals heaved forward, dragging their bundles and children toward us, toward the gangplank. Soldiers lashed out to keep them at bay, whipping the crowds with long knotted ropes as we boarded.

The light. That's what I remember of my view from the ferry's bow, how daylight suddenly seemed so much brighter, how sunlight dappled the river's swells like diamonds tossed down from the sky. Ten miles across at its widest, the river's broad vista unfolded before me, promising to take me away. So mighty and meandering, this river, this vein of life. So much history was written on its banks, so much misery. It filled me with regret to be leaving this way. I'd come to love Kinshasa for its vibrance, but I felt tingly, almost light-headed, that my escape was finally at hand.

BAM! The troops opened fire. The *ratatatatatat* ricocheted over the river. It seemed to come from everywhere. I hit the deck, crouching low. My traveling colleagues did likewise. I didn't know who was shooting or why. I chanced a quick glance up to the port in time to see the troops spraying their AK-47s like water hoses to stop the desperate locals who'd rushed the boat. The throng of bodies and bundles hit the ground. Oh God, oh Jesus. Don't let them be dead. Please don't drop another mass killing at my feet. I wanted the entire scene to go away. I wanted no responsibility for it. Emotionally exhausted, I did not want to care.

I could not take any more.

I'd called myself "Duke of Africa" once upon a time. Back when I felt expansive and full of wonder at the start of my tour as a foreign correspondent. I'd made up the name to sign off e-mails to my editors back in Washington. I liked its dashing sound and knew they'd get a kick out of it, too.

And I did feel grand. I loved my work. I loved living in Africa—the way it felt, so foreign but familiar, so much another world, and yet a world that was my heritage. I was, after all, rare: a black American woman foreign correspondent. I was seasoned in my field, arriving in Africa after eight years with the *Washington Post*, and the independence of foreign journalism, the freedom to roam and write, ranked for me as the most privileged perch a reporter could find. I milked it to the fullest.

I descended deep underground in South Africa and Zambia, into gold and copper mines that kept economies afloat. I lunched on a Congo River speedboat cruise with diamond merchants from Britain and Belgium and felt the sting of the First World's long tentacles manipulating economies of the Third World. I jousted with cabinet ministers in interviews that became debates, sometimes exposing my own frustration with African policies that made no sense, other times commiserating with the awful hand that Africa had been dealt. For no good reason—yes, there were times when I had no mission—I paddled the Zambezi River, dodging its hippos in a comic fiasco I will never forget and in which others less fortunate than I have died. On another journey, I slept in a pup tent in a remote Namibian village where crops were plagued by elephants, and cattle were targeted by lions.

Women called me "sister." Elderly men called me "daughter." Children in dusty, rough-hewn villages gathered round just to watch a foreigner and giggle. Their delight was mine. I was the American, the black American, a source of fascination, answering as many questions as I asked. People wanted to know about our civil rights struggle. Our jazz and rap. Our American racism. Our superstars. I felt like a messenger from the other side of the vast ocean that separated us physically but also linked us.

I absorbed Africa's generous humanity and fell in love with it.

On my journeys, people begged me for money, for help, for food. It unnerved me, always, to stand in the midst of such suffering and be unable to offer relief. I tried to help in small ways when I could, and I harbored the naive hope that, at the least, my dispatches could bring understanding to a world that so often viewed Africa grimly, so wrongly.

WHOOPI GOLDBERG *is the chosen name of the fiercely funny comedienne who was born Caryn Johnson. Crowned by her signature dreadlocks, Whoopi has appeared in over forty movies and has dozens of acting and producing credits to her name in theater and television—not bad for a ninth-grade dropout. When she won an Oscar—for best supporting actress—in 1991, she was only the second black woman to win the coveted award and the fifth African American. In 2001 she was presented with the Kennedy Center Mark Twain Prize for American Humor.*

Choices

It was just me and my mother and Clyde, in our little apartment in Chelsea. When I was little, my mother was a nurse at French Hospital, and later on she became one of the best Head Start teachers in New York City. We took our little trips. The Circle Line. The Statue of Liberty. Coney Island was the best, though. Coming out of the subway tunnel in Manhattan and shooting into the hot, open light of Brooklyn was the most exciting thing. It was like alighting in a foreign territory. And then, finally, the doors would open at Coney Island and I'd be hit by that smell: caramel apples, popcorn, hot dogs. It washed over me, and I was gone.

But as cool as it was to head out for Coney Island, just the three of us, or to the Statue of Liberty, or the movies, it was even cooler coming home. To have *been* there was somehow sweeter than actually being there, you know. And to come home and tell the other kids about the adventure, to reclaim our own little world, where everyone knew everyone else, where there was no such thing as rich or poor, where we belonged, well, this was the greatest thing of all.

Here's what I know: Folks at the bottom rungs are

having a tough time pulling themselves up to a better place, and folks up top aren't always reaching down to lend a helping hand. I've been at both ends of the ladder. I lived on welfare, as a young mother, and there was no shame in it for me. I'm actually proud of what I was able to do for me and my kid, and I'm not fool enough to think I could have done it on my own. I didn't come to the welfare system without first putting into it. I had all kinds of jobs as a kid. I paid my taxes, and I did so thinking the money would be working for me, for when I needed it.

When I was a young mom, I left New York for Texas, to join a friend of mine and work as a nanny to his one-year-old kid. It seemed like a good fit. Our kids were the same age, and I liked taking care of children. When my friend moved out to California I took my daughter and moved out with him. It was a good situation, but like most good things it eventually soured, and I found myself in a strange new place with no money to get back home. I couldn't drive, and even if I could drive I didn't have the money for a car, and I had no skills except for some after-school program stuff I could do with kids, so I was screwed coming and going and staying. I had no high school diploma. I had me, and my kid.

And so I turned to my last, best hope, and started collecting the welfare money I was entitled to. I took the money and kept looking for a job. I was willing to try anything. One guy taught me to lay brick, and I was out there laying bricks and cement and doing all this masonry with my little girl at my side. She came with me every day. She's got her handprints somewhere at the San Diego Zoo. Me, I get famous and leave my prints in the cement outside Grauman's Chinese Theatre, and she gets the San Diego Zoo.

After that I met some folks who needed a hair model for their cosmetology school. It was pretty boring, just sitting there like that, and I started to think it'd be interesting to be the one doing stuff to the hair, and the folks running the place were kind enough to give me a scholarship. They taught you hair care, skin care, nail care, foot care. It was the whole beauty school package, the works.

I got to be a fairly decent stylist, but then I went to work for a funeral home, working on dead people. It was actually one of the all-time OK jobs. The money was good; you made your own hours; you were left to yourself, pretty much; and the customer rarely talked back. I did makeup, hair, the whole thing, and I could take my kid with me and she wouldn't make too much trouble.

The guy I went out to San Diego with was a theater

person, and through him I started hanging out with all these other theater people, and after a while I started trying to get them to hire me—to act, to do hair or makeup—for whatever production they were working on. If you got the gig, the San Diego Repertory Company paid like $25 per week. The work was sporadic but when you're a single mom, doing what you can to put a reasonable meal on the table, an extra twenty-five bucks goes a long way.

We lived in a nice house, in a canyon, in the trees. It was out of a storybook, this place. We were literally on top of the trees, with two giant trunks growing up through the deck. There was a bedroom, a living room, and a kitchen, all for $77 per month. It was the first house I ever lived in, and I used to sit out on my deck at the end of a tough day and look out over the canyon and think what the future might hold. It really was a special place.

I've heard my mother come out of my mouth more often than I ever could have imagined. It wasn't supposed to be that way. Well, please. You'll shake your finger or throw your hands on your hips, same as your mother did, and suddenly you're looking at your own face and thinking, Look what I've become—a fax of my folks.

One night when my kid was maybe thirteen or fourteen, she came downstairs wearing three pieces of cloth. She said she was going out, and it was none of my business where. I looked this child over, this little version of me. The cloth itself was all shiny and nice and fine, but it wasn't covering enough to suit a mother. OK, in my time I wore a mini so small that all I needed to do was sneeze and you would have known exactly what color my panties were, but here was my barely teenage daughter, looking like a grown woman. I completely flipped.

I'm trying to explain to this child that she can't go out looking like this because you don't know what invitation someone is going to pick up from this. That line—you don't know what invitation someone is going to pick up from this—was one of my mother's, and I wanted to suck it right back into my face as soon as I'd said it. I reconnected to everything that had passed between my mother and me, and I could see what was coming. I wanted to tell my mother how sorry I was for putting her through all these emotions, for not recognizing that she had something to offer beyond what I could see.

I turned to my kid and said, "You know what? Go out. Just go."

And she did. She looked at me kinda funny, and

suspicious, but she went out like she'd planned. And then she came back, about twenty minutes later. "You know what?" she said. "It's cold out there. I think I'm gonna change, put a little more on."

Kids can shake your beliefs right down to their foundations. My fourteen-year-old called me up on the phone one day. I was on location. I picked up and she said, "Mom, I'm pregnant." Just like that.

I sucked in the deepest breath I could find, realized she wasn't kidding. This was the last thing I expected to hear from my kid. She had all the information she needed to keep herself from getting pregnant. We had talked. She had understood. And yet here she was, pregnant.

My initial response seemed so obvious I didn't even see the need to give it voice. I didn't think this was one of those times I could leave my daughter to come to her own decision. This was just something we had to do. She was fourteen. She wasn't equipped to raise a kid. Emotionally, financially, practically . . . she just wasn't equipped. And I didn't want to raise her kid for her.

"Mom?" She wasn't finished, apparently. "I want to keep this baby," she said quietly. Not exactly asking me, but telling me. It was so totally not what I was expecting to hear. The first piece was a shock, and this latest was off the Richter scale.

I still hadn't said anything and now I didn't dare. I realized that if I was out there screaming to preserve a woman's right to an abortion, I was also out there preserving my daughter's right *not* to have an abortion. I had to take my beliefs out for a little test drive, because pro-choice means pro-choice, right? It means women (and fourteen-year-old girls) have the choice to do whatever they want. And here it was my daughter's choice to keep this child. OK, fine. It bumped smack into what my choice would have been for her, but that is what she wanted.

I'm glad this was what she wanted, because I like my grandkid. She's great. She was born on my birthday. Most kids give you a watch or a wallet on your birthday, or some flowers, but my daughter gave me a living, breathing human being. She also gave me a lesson. She taught me that "pro-choice" is not just a phrase.

Life is precious. Absolutely. All I need is to hold my grandkid in my arms and the argument is made. I've even got another one now, so it's just precious times two. My daughter had a second child when she was about twenty-two, and her two children are just heaven. She's married now, to a great guy, and doing just fine. So don't go hollerin' at me that life is precious. I know. But I also know that freedom and responsibility are precious things, and that if we run out of either, we're screwed.

How many times do you have to open the newspaper to get the point? Every week, it seems there's another story about a young mother abandoning her unwanted child in some Dumpster, somewhere. Rich or poor, it doesn't matter. If it keeps happening it means someone, somewhere is dropping the ball.

So let's get it straight: Pro-choice means you can go either way. If you get pregnant, decide what you want to do. Do you want to have this child? Are you able to have this child? Will you be able to finish school, or get a job, or look forward to any kind of productive future? You should decide on these things *before* you go out and get pregnant, but I realize that's probably asking too much. Think it through and decide, and if you decide not to have the child, you should be able to have a clean, safe abortion, with dignity and respect. We were lucky in our house, and it worked out, but this ain't supposed to be about luck.

I can do anything. I can be anything. No one ever told me I couldn't. No one ever expressed this idea that I was limited to any one thing, and so I think in terms of what's possible, not impossible.

Movies were my first window to the outside world, and they told me I could go anywhere, be whatever I wanted, solve any puzzle. The right movie was my ticket to any place I wanted to go. But it had to be the right movie, and it had to come from the right place, 'cause I had to bank on it being historically accurate. You couldn't always trust the history books. They told a diluted truth. In movies too. They didn't always get the story right, especially when it came to our nonwhite history.

Movies opened doors to a lot of things for me, but for every one they opened another one closed. The casting always messed with the way I saw it. In this way, books were more liberating, more magical, and so I started to read. To really *read*. Books opened the mind to all kinds of possibilities. There is nothing in Dickens to leave you thinking there were no black people in England, or that Bob Cratchit didn't pass you on the street every single day. But movies made you believe there were no black people. When I was little, this didn't strike me as off, but as I grew up, it bothered me. I knew there had to be more to us than that.

This—the possibility—is why I look on acting as such a

joyous thing. Anything can happen. I believed I could pass as an ancient Roman in *A Funny Thing Happened on the Way to the Forum*. I believed a little girl could rise from a single-parent household in the Manhattan projects, start a single-parent household of her own, struggle through seven years of welfare and odd jobs, and still wind up making movies. You can go from anonymity to Planet Hollywood and never lose sight of where you've been.

So, yeah, I think anything is possible. I know it because I have lived it. I know it because I have seen it. I have witnessed things the ancients would have called miracles, but they are not miracles. They are the products of someone's dream, and they happen as the result of hard work. If something hasn't happened, it's not because it can't happen, or won't; it just hasn't happened yet.

E. LYNN HARRIS *is the best-selling author of nine novels—
at last count—that total more than 3 million copies in print.
After he graduated from the University of Arkansas at Fay-
etteville, he worked as a computer sales executive for more
than a decade. But success in the business world could barely
camouflage the deep depression he felt living without love
and honesty inside a sexual closet. By coming out as a gay
man and writing popular, appealing stories, Harris has
freed himself—and liberated many of his readers from prej-
udice as well.*

The Power of Words

As a child I loved to read, but I had no desire to be a writer. I wanted to be a teacher. Once, when I was eleven, I was playing school with the neighborhood kids on our front porch. Daddy came storming out of the house and shouted in front of all the children assembled, "Only sissy boys want to be schoolteachers." Then he kicked all my books and fake report cards off the porch and gave me an *I dare you to go get them* look. Daddy's beatings caused me to retreat into my own silent world.

I had strange notions about life and God. One of the strangest had to do with the power of words. I was convinced that at the beginning of your life you were given a set number of words to utter and when you used them up you died. Words were powerful, I thought, and must be used wisely. When I had to speak, I would count the number of words in my head and eliminate those words that were not necessary. I would look at my mother and sisters in disbelief when they would talk needlessly. Didn't they know what I knew?

A few months before my twelfth birthday, I decided death was better than my life with Daddy, and I began to talk excessively. I would read books out loud, even though I was so proud of the fact that I had learned to read silently before anyone in my class. My constant jabbering got me in trouble not only at home but at school as well.

On my twelfth birthday, I was terribly sad when the day ended and I was still in the land of the living. My family didn't understand why I was so sad, since birthdays in our home had always been joyous events. I didn't tell anyone why I was brokenhearted; I felt empowered by my secret knowledge about God, words, and death.

A couple of weeks later, something happened that made me happy I'd stayed around.

Jean was our "play" cousin. Our families had known each other since the first day we moved into the neighborhood in Little Rock, Arkansas. Jean said something that would change my life, words that would release Daddy's power over me.

"You know, maybe he's not even your real daddy."

I asked Jean what she meant. Jean said confidently that no father would treat a son the way Ben treated me.

Such a thought had never crossed my mind. I was wondering how I could find out if Jean was right without asking my mother and risking another whipping, when the picture of Mama's gray cardboard box entered my mind.

The box housed all of our family's important papers and was hidden in Mama's closet.

I told Jean about the box, and minutes later I found myself on her narrow shoulders, reaching for it amid Mama's shoes and hatboxes. When I located the box I grabbed it too quickly, and I fell from Jean's shoulders to the floor. The box flew from my hands and crashed down beside me.

I quickly started rummaging through the stack of papers, looking for my birth certificate. When we reached the bottom of the box, I suddenly saw a black piece of paper covered with white ink.

I saw my name, "Everette Lynn," and then my eyes scanned over the rest of my document when suddenly Jean said, "Look here, where it says 'father's name.'"

My eyes followed her slender finger to the spot and I saw the name "Jeter." My father was James Jeter and not Ben Harris. But who was James Jeter? I wanted to cry, but I felt a happiness inside that I had never known.

I read that I had actually been born in Michigan, and not Arkansas as I'd always thought.

"Uncle Ben's not your daddy. Now we know why he treats you the way he does."

My discovery didn't stop the beatings and verbal abuse.

But my secret information provided me with an omnipotent shield that protected me. When I was thirteen, my mother divorced Ben. Divorce was a rare occurrence in our community and was considered grown folks' business. I became the man of the house, helping my mother take care of our home and my sisters.

At the end of my sophomore year in high school, Mama sent me to Flint, Michigan, for the summer, to stay with my Uncle Clarence Allen and his five children. I think she thought it would be good for me to be around boys my own age and experience the fatherly influence my uncle could provide. One day I was alone in the normally busy house washing dishes. This was different for me, because my mother had never assigned me chores that were considered women's work. But I didn't complain, since none of the Allen boys seemed to think there was anything wrong with doing housework.

Just as I was rinsing out one of the last glasses, I glanced out of the kitchen window and saw a stranger who locked his car door and started to walk across the street toward the house with my uncle. An eerie feeling washed over me. I noticed how much the stranger looked like me. I immediately thought, *Could this man be my father?*

I heard my uncle's footsteps as he called out my name: "Lynn? Is Lynn here?"

I moved slowly to the hallway and was suddenly standing face-to-face with my uncle and the stranger.

"Do you know who I am?" he asked.

"No, sir," I lied.

"I'm your daddy," he said. "Didn't your mama tell you 'bout me?"

"No, sir." As far as I knew, my mother didn't know that I knew the secret she kept hidden in the gray box. For a moment, the three of us stood close together. Then, without warning, I suddenly darted between them and bolted down the stairs and burst through the screen door and ran.

I had dreamed so many nights about my father and what it would be like to meet him. I fantasized that he would take me away from Little Rock and allow me to live with him, that he would teach me how to be a man. Now that the time had come, it wasn't at all like my dreams. I wanted to be happy, but I felt a sadness shadowing me. Why had I run away from him? What was I afraid of?

Maybe he would think I was a sissy, as Ben had. So I was a bit surprised by the flash of joy I experienced the

next day when my father returned with a look of determination on his handsome face. He walked toward me and
asked if we could talk. He then told me some very exciting
news. I had some brothers and sisters anxious to meet me.
This was too good to be true. Suddenly I wasn't afraid.

Before the summer ended and I returned to Little Rock,
I visited my father's house several times. I loved my brothers and sisters. My father's wife was easy to talk to and told
me it was OK for me not to feel totally comfortable with
my father, that our relationship would come with time.

My mind was filled with so many questions. Like why
didn't he marry my mother? Why didn't he visit? Why had
he waited until I was almost an adult to show up?

My questions for my father were never answered. I
never had the opportunity to ask them. The father I never
really knew was killed before I could return to Flint the
following summer. The victim of a drunk driver, my father was killed instantly when a car in which he was a pas-
senger collided with a parked eighteen-wheel truck.

What I did after my father's death was what I had done
before I met him. I depended on my fantasy father, who
could be whatever I wanted him to be. I never saw my
brothers and sisters again after that summer.

I finally had to acknowledge to myself that my feelings toward men were not like those of most boys my age.

I was on my way to Washington, D.C. An exclusive program was bringing low-income African American high school students from around the country to work. I arrived safely at George Washington University, where the participants would be staying for the six-week program. We would work half-days at government agencies and spend the rest of our time attending classes on things like etiquette, and sightseeing in the nation's capital and surrounding areas.

During the first day of orientation, one of the counselors warned boys in the program to be careful because Washington had a huge gay problem. *Gay problem?* Curious, I raised my hand, and asked, "What is gay?"

The room roared with laughter. Here I was, this hick from Arkansas asking what gay was. The director had a puzzled look on her face as she glanced toward one of the male counselors for help.

A participant from Omaha, Nebraska, a big football player type, stopped his laughter long enough to look at me and say, "Punks, sissies. Boys who want to be girls. I know y'all got them down South."

"Oh," I said, embarrassed. So that's what I was. *Gay.* Part of a problem.

It didn't matter how many girls I dated or how many lies I told. My infatuations with men were going to cause major problems for me. Yet I couldn't call myself gay. I felt a great deal of shame. I knew that being gay and not accepting it was going to destroy me. I've heard that people who take pills in suicide attempts really don't want to die, but just want attention. All I know is that taking pills was the only way I knew how to kill myself. I wanted to die. No matter what I tried to do, I just couldn't bring myself out of my ocean-deep depression.

It was time for some new dreams. I had spent so much of my life following what I have come to know as my rain dreams: the ones that I could hear, those I thought the world wanted for me, like being married and successful in my career. But the dream of writing was becoming powerful and silent, like snow. It was one of the few times that I listened to myself without worrying about what others would think. I saw that just like snow, writing could provide me comfort.

I originally set out to write a story for me, because I realized I might be the only one who would read it. I wanted to write a story that would capture the pain and joy of being black and gay. I wanted it to be a love story, because the one problem I had with admitting that I was gay was that I had to give up having true love like in the movies.

Since my dream of being a writer was coming in the form of images of snow, my first scene was a beautiful winter night when the main character, Raymond, and his lover, Kelvin, meet and frolic in the snow after Christmas. In real life, a situation like this had happened with me. I wanted my story to be one where women, if they decided to read it, would think about the choices they made when it came to men. After my first night at the computer, I found myself looking forward to the next day when I could return to my new friends. I was amazed at how these characters were coming to life in my head.

Writing and getting my novel published became my new therapy. When people asked me what I did for a living, I said I was a writer. I had never felt so self-confident about my future. The confidence didn't disappear even when I had a stack of rejection letters almost as big as my novel. I was getting emotional and financial support from family and friends. The mere fact that they didn't look at me like I was crazy when I said I was writing a book about gay and bisexual men was support enough.

After finishing the book, I decided that if the New York

publishers didn't think my book was good enough to publish, then I would do it myself. I became a one-man publishing company. I couldn't wait until some editor in New York discovered my novel. I would have to take a chance.

I was beginning to believe that the novel would have an impact not only on my life but on my family and other families like mine. One night while talking to my Aunt Gee, who has always been supportive of me, she said something that hurt me deeply.

"Baby, if I had raised you, I don't think you would have been gay."

"No, Aunt Gee, you're wrong. I might have learned to love myself sooner, but I still would have been gay."

I knew she didn't mean any harm, nor did she understand that she was implying that my being gay was a product of my environment. This is a very common misperception, even today.

The next day, I delivered a copy of my novel to my aunt. A couple of days later I got a call from her.

"Baby, I just finished your novel, and it's beautiful. Will you please forgive me for what I said the other day? Now I finally understand what you were trying to tell me."

Through my tears I told her that of course I could forgive her and thanked her for calling.

Writing has allowed me to craft and sculpt a magnificent life and touch the lives of others in ways that still awe and humble me. Every day I receive e-mails from fans who let me know how much my books mean to them, and how their lives have been enriched and changed. Writing is my lifeline. Writing saved my life.

SISTER SOULJAH *is a cultural warrior, writer, and community activist who speaks her truth with intelligence, perception, and what she herself calls "a spicy attitude." Born Lisa Williamson, she studied at Cornell and at Spain's University of Salamanca while still in high school. After graduating from Rutgers University, she traveled all over the United States, Europe, and Africa. Souljah often uses her platform to analyze the complex legacy of slavery, focusing on confused relationships in which love can feel like a form of war. Her second book,* The Coldest Winter Ever, *a novel, was published in 1999 and became a bestseller.*

Lessons

I was excited to be going to college. After all, college is the one place on earth that offers young people the chance to be free. By living on campus, far from home, we get the opportunity to act out all of our suppressed personality traits and hidden desires. We then become the person we've always wanted to be. College offered me the opportunity to select my own courses, my own professors, my own direction. College would free me sexually as well.

My first day in my new college dormitory room I stood in front of my mirror, admiring my long eyelashes, my big brown eyes, broad shoulders, full titties, small waist, and baby-making hips. I knew that this body was a weapon, but I also considered it to be sacred—something that I would give and share only with one special person.

Don't get me wrong. I was as "hot" as any other young woman.

The only difference was that in high school, all of my sexual affairs happened inside my mind. I had steamy fantasies about certain brothers whom I considered to be strong—men who would have never thought that I'd be thinking of them in that way because I had deliberately misled them with my intelligent ways. But everything would change now, because at college I would be with thousands of anonymous people and hundreds of black men to choose from. I was sure that at least one of them would like me.

I had a class called "Black Education." For the first time, I had a professor, a black man, admit that racism was and still is a monumental problem that plagues America. Instead of having the usual discussion of whether racism existed or whether it was a figment of the imagination of over 30 million black people, we had a full exploration of its forms and manifestations.

After class I rushed to the college bookstore. While searching the shelves of African studies, I got sidetracked by the many interesting books that were available. I was overwhelmed and angry at the same time. Overwhelmed, because here was a wealth of knowledge I hadn't known about. Angry, because my high school teachers were either completely ignorant, or had hidden this information from me. Overwhelmed, because I intended to read all of these books.

As I was flipping through the pages of Carter G. Woodson's *Mis-Education of the Negro*, a tall, very dark-skinned brother with a closely cropped beard stood in front of me and said, "Read it! Every college student should." He held out his hand to me and introduced himself: "Nathan."

I told him my name and he invited me for a drink. When I told him I didn't drink alcohol, he said, "Excuse me, I didn't realize you were still a baby."

I calmly said, "So, how old are you, old man?"

"Twenty-four, senior, political science/history double major."

I reached up, grabbed my copy of *Institutional Racism*, and said, "Peace, take it easy."

I read the book like a starving man would eat a fish sandwich. Each sentence prompted a new thought and I began connecting each thought to the things that had happened in my life or to the people I loved. I began to understand about my community, how it was organized, how it was not organized, and how it got to be so miserable in the first place.

As the semester came to a close, I knew I had grown both intellectually and spiritually. I had learned the valuable lesson that the more you think you know, the less you know. The more willing you are to learn, the more likely you are to seek and find only to discover that there is still so much more. Although I longed for companionship, I discovered so much comfort and peace of mind in my newfound books, I continued my self-examination. I used Carter Woodson's book to begin to address my eighteen years of mis-education.

One day while I was cramming for my upcoming English exam, up walked Nathan. "Listen, I stay up late and live in your building on the third floor. Come check me out, we'll talk and listen to some music."

"What do you take me for, freshman meat?"

"No, don't bug out. It's just that we all finish our work late. Anyway you won't be the only one there. Come on down and kick it with us tonight."

Later that night I debated whether I should go see Nathan. I was bored. I put on baggy pants and an over-sized sweatshirt so I would look as unsexy as possible. I didn't want him to get the wrong impression, and, frankly, I didn't feel attracted to him. I was going for the conversation, which I had discovered was hard to come by.

As I approached Nathan's door I heard voices and could smell incense. I was relieved other people were there. They had been talking about Middle Eastern politics, debating who was wrong and who was right. The hour was late but my eyes were wide as plums. I was thrilled because I hardly ever met people who were serious about learning and understanding issues, people who support their arguments with intricate details backed up by books on the topic. I felt embarrassed because I had assumed Nathan was sweating me and just wanted some pussy. Instead, it felt like an honor to be in his presence, to listen to his voice, and to be able to share in his wealth of knowledge.

The university gave us nearly five-and-a-half weeks' vacation. I kept hoping Nathan would call. I began to look up a few of my old high school acquaintances just to kill time. One day the phone rang. Nathan asked, "You wanna hang out in New York with me?" I said softly, "Sure, why not."

We went to Manhattan's Lower East Side and he showed me the little news shops where political and economic journals from around the world could be bought. He cautioned me about trusting the media. He said they attempted to shape public opinion and went so far as to create "facts" to lie to the people in the interest of maintaining their own power. Later, we went up to the Metropolitan Museum of Art, which had a limited holiday engagement of "Treasures of Ancient Egypt." Nathan explained everything that he said the tour guide had "left out." He ended my lesson by telling me that the reason the exhibit was called Egyptian and not African was because white scholars wanted the world to believe that the Egyptians were non-African. This they did so African people would feel we had contributed nothing to civilization.

Leaving the museum, we went to a health food restaurant to have dinner. Nathan smiled and said, "I brought you here because you were starting to look like 'two tons of fun.'" My heart stood still as I realized that I had gained twenty pounds since starting college.

After dinner, Nathan put me on a bus that would take me back to New Jersey. He didn't try to kiss me, which was cool, because I didn't feel comfortable yet. Just before I got on the bus, he said, "You know, you're a beautiful girl, but we have to work on you. I've always wondered why you have that fake extra piece of hair weaved in the back of your head. Does it give you that much more of a sense of security and value?"

I was astounded. Nobody had ever mentioned my weave. I had always acted as if it were my own hair. How could he be so insensitive? "All I'm saying is, I think *your* hair is beautiful." I smiled meekly and got on the bus.

The next day I went to the store and bought an exercise album. Then I went to get my own hair braided into a natural style. For four and a half weeks, I exercised rigorously. It wasn't hard to reform and I was looking damn good for my return to the university. The odd thing was that Nathan had never called me back since the day we spent together. I blamed myself and my appearance for his disappearance.

All during the first two weeks of our new semester I didn't hear from Nathan. I dealt with my disappointment by working extra hard in my new classes. Who was this man I was not initially attracted to, but was now mentally entrapped by? Why did he occupy so much of my thoughts?

I was awakened by the sound of whispers. My digital clock said it was 3:30 in the morning. I sat up and saw my roommate Mona talking softly through a semi-cracked-open door with the chain lock still in place.

Oh my God, it was Nathan. I put on my robe. I unchained the door, stepped into the dimly lit dormitory hall, and folded my arms in front of me.

"Yes, Nathan?" I said with a firm sensuality.

His big brown eyes filled with both a physical and spiritual glow. Then he said, "Man, I'm into you. No more frontin'. I can't deny it. Your brain got me going but it's scary. You're too powerful. Even when you don't see me you have my attention. Your spirit is so strong it's like an invasion." Nathan's words came gushing out.

"Nathan, I know you can feel that I want you. But I want you on my terms. I don't want to play games. I'm in it for keeps. Not for a night or a couple of weeks."

"Don't you think I know that? That's why I've been running for weeks. I didn't know there were any women like you, so you caught me off guard. I can't stay. I just wanted you to know that I'm here."

A week passed by and no sign of Nathan. I thought to myself, "Oh, he's still running." That night I knocked on Nathan's door. He opened with the usual warm smile. I closed the door behind me and put the chain lock on. Nathan's room was a careful arrangement of dim lights and candles, incense and jazz.

Then, smiling, he said, "There's something special about you, girl, something spiritual and uncorrupted, something pure. That's why I ran from you. Because I know you are directly from God and I don't want to hurt you." He turned off the lights and only the candle flickered in the darkness. As he undid his clothes I noticed for the first time what I believed a real man looked like. I was young and fascinated. For the first time I felt secure, my body bursting with pleasure as his lips offered me a comfort, warmth, and power I had never known.

I woke up the next morning to shades wide open, springtime sun beaming, and an empty bed. Nathan was gone. A brief frenzy led me to a note that Nathan had left on his desktop. It said, "Peace. You're deep and natural. Don't worry, you'll get yours in a box." I quickly concluded that he felt I was special and that that feeling would one day lead him to offer me an engagement ring, because rings came in a box.

Nathan graduated. He was my man and I was his woman. As May turned into June and June turned into July, Nathan became cranky and short on patience. He'd come home from his job search amazed that people were asking him if he could type, play football, coach a team, or drive a truck. He seemed distraught, discouraged, and depressed.

Friday afternoon I got to Nathan's house a little earlier than expected and he had a guest. He seemed so upbeat from his usual unemployed funk that I knew this must be somebody important. He introduced the brother to me and said that he was his "old running partner," his "partner in crime," the brother who had "taught me everything I know today." I was impressed. David seemed even more polished than Nathan but that was to be expected since he was, after all, Nathan's "teacher."

Nathan signaled me to come into the kitchen. "Baby, do you mind if we change our date until tomorrow night? I haven't seen Dave in over a year and he's telling me about a job he has lined up for me at an advertising firm." I was so happy. I gave Nathan a kiss and said, "I'll see you tomorrow then, baby. Good luck!"

Tomorrow came but Nathan never did.

Seventy days, seventy prayers, and twenty-five lost pounds later, I received a call. "I need you, please come. I need you."

Two hours later I walked through a crowded bar filled with men and women dressed in business-style suits, laughing, drinking, and smoking. I found Nate bellying up to the bar. He had obviously been drinking for several hours.

"Nate! What's going on?"

"I got the job!"

"Well, I can see that. What else is going on? Why did

you leave me, Nate? I don't understand this. We were strong when we were together. Where did you go that weekend?"

His laugh was a harsh and bitter bark. "I was with my lover, David! He helped me get this way, you know. I tried to fight the demons but no matter what I did and how hard I tried the demons kept coming back."

The blood seemed to empty from my body and spill all over the floor. I sat lifeless for what seemed an eternity. Old scenes of love, prayer, respect, education, and mutual history flashed through my brain. There was no longer any relationship to fix. It was just one human being helping a dirty, drunk, and confused human being out of a bar before some tragedy came upon him.

I took him back to my room and laid him on my bed, where he fell fast asleep. I grabbed the chair, where I slept until morning. When I awoke the room was filled with silence and shame.

"So . . . Nate is gay."

"No! I never use that term. I love women. I love you. I think you're beautiful. But I'm sick. I'll be fine for months and then when the pressure mounts up, the feeling comes back again. When I met you, you were a change and a challenge. I could pretend that 'my problem' was under control. Women made that easy. They were empty-headed and had no self-respect. All I had to do was keep pointing out their faults so they would never see my faults. Then you came along. I couldn't find any angles. I was genuinely turned on. But I was confused so I tried to stay away. I prayed for strength and direction, still knowing I wasn't the man that you deserved. That's why I left."

"So, I was like an experiment for you."

"No, I wouldn't say that. Believe me, I am not gay. My feelings were and still are real. I have to repair myself before I can unite with someone as sure and true as you are. So I freed you because I love you."

I sat motionless trying to digest all Nathan was confessing to me. I was no longer attracted to him. He now sat before me a shattered husk of a man.

"But, Nate," I said, "you lied to me. That's the thing that hurts me most."

Nate stood up and slowly collected his few things. "If people lie to God each and every day, in their prayers, in their promises, and in their actions, what makes you think they won't lie to you?"

MICHAEL COTTMAN, *a news journalist and political writer, is also an avid scuba diver. He combined his two passions—writing and diving—to research the history of the Henrietta Marie, a British slave ship that disappeared in 1700. The shipwreck was identified off the Florida Keys in 1983. Thousands of its artifacts, including iron shackles and elephant tusks, are on exhibit at the Mel Fisher Maritime Heritage Society in Key West. Cottman was part of a team of black divers determined to honor their African ancestors in a unique way.*

History at Sea

They emerged from the sea dripping salt water, their rubber suits squeaking, their tanned, dark features barely visible inside the round masks pressed against their faces. A dozen men with bulky ribbed hoses dangling from their shoulders, steel tanks strapped to their backs, and knives fastened to their legs appeared from deep below the ocean's surface.

They had descended into the depths, chasing wide-winged stingrays that glided by just out of reach; they had come face to face with sleek sharks that zigzagged out of the shadows and vanished as quickly as they appeared; they had seen a school of rainbow runners shifting silently with the rhythm of the sea, the most entertaining choreography they had ever witnessed.

And in the eerie silence of the sea, where hand signals replace speech, the measured thumping of their heartbeats had been amplified, sounding like the thunder of African drums.

On a sunny winter morning in Fort Lauderdale, in November of 1991, nearly 150 African American divers began arriving at the first convention by cars, trains, and airplanes, unsure of what they were going to find but somehow having the knowledge that they were going to be part of something remarkably special and historically significant.

Black divers from across the country strolled into the hotel, shook hands, and introduced themselves. Divers from the same cities, who lived blocks apart, were meeting one another for the first time, tales of big fish were being swapped, and divers were holding discussions about the ever-evolving scuba gear and the latest in technology.

But there was one refrain that seemed to echo throughout the hotel: *"I never knew there were so many black divers!"*

Many of the divers were talking about exotic locations and the ever-exhilarating shark dives when Dr. Jose Jones entered the room to deliver his first speech as cofounder of the National Association of Black Scuba Divers (NABS). They were doctors and lawyers, policemen and firefighters, educators and computer executives, chemists and engineers, postal workers and architects.

Dr. Jones spoke of winters past, of cultural connections, of links to our African forefathers.

"There's a ship not far from here, a slave ship called the

Henrietta Marie, a ship that carried our ancestors from Africa to the West Indies three hundred years ago," Jones said. "It carried some of your family members and it carried some of mine. This is an extraordinary opportunity—and the first opportunity—for black scuba divers to study a slave ship that represents a portion of our history.

"What I would like to see is some kind of plaque—or memorial—placed at the site of the *Henrietta Marie*. A commemoration from black people, black divers, to black people, African people, our people, that we can leave on the ocean floor."

What Jones was proposing was unparalleled. Never before had a group of black scuba divers honored their African ancestors in such a way.

"This is an opportunity of a lifetime and we can't let it slip away," he said. Jones suggested a monument be placed on the site of the *Henrietta Marie* the following year, when the organization would meet in Key West.

All sorts of questions raced through his mind: How much should such a monument weigh to stay in place? How long would it take to get it to the wreck site? How much would it cost? How many divers would it take to lower it to the bottom? What about the strong currents?

Oswald Sykes, a former water-safety instructor, proved to be the logical choice to head the committee. He spent hours each day researching information about how to construct a monument and lower it into the sea, the best methods for adding bronze inscription, boat costs, weather patterns, and licenses and approvals by the Florida marine, environmental, and coast guard officials.

I had decided to write a feature story for New York *Newsday* about NABS and the dive on a slave ship that no one in New York—or the rest of the country—had heard anything about.

It was November 1992. The weather that day was lousy—gray skies, heavy rain, and wild winds. We couldn't have picked worse weather if we had planned it. The forecast called for the weather to clear in five days—just in time to head home.

On any other occasion, I would have been sulking because I had traveled for a dive trip and couldn't dive. But on this day, the weather didn't bother me. I was caught up in the excitement of meeting other African American divers, people who would change my life in some measurable way, and rotten weather wasn't going to interfere with something that was destined to be.

The next morning, we learned that fifteen-mile-an-hour winds were blowing five-foot swells around the reefs. We took a straw poll, and against our better judgment, we headed out to sea.

We saw adventure up close. Sheets of rain were falling hard. We bounced to the dive site in about twenty minutes. As we strapped on our tanks and slipped into fins, the rain seemed to let up just a bit. We thought our luck was changing, so we took a quick poll and about half of us hard-core divers decided to make the dive.

The visibility had gotten worse. We lost sight of the anchor line within seconds of our descent and a monster current was sweeping us away from the boat and out to sea before we could get our bearings underwater.

Things were happening fast. My dive buddies, Rachel Scott, a bank executive from North Carolina, and Rosalyn Woolfolk, a businesswoman from Atlanta, were floating with me in about fifteen feet of silty sea, unable to place the anchor line and riding a strong current in the wrong direction. At about fifty feet, the current vanished.

We swam and kicked constantly. We were sucking up air and we knew that we had a long way to go. Rachel and Rosalyn cupped their hands together, the hand signal that means, "Where is the boat?"

Five minutes later, Rachel yanked my fin and showed

me her pressure gauge; the needle was inching toward empty. She was getting very low on air, and so was I.

We ascended slowly to about twenty feet and swam for three minutes as a safety measure. I instructed them to stay at that depth while I swam to the surface to see if we were anywhere close to the boat.

As my head broke the surface, rain was falling hard and the current was knocking me against the waves.

I did a 360-degree spin, searching for the boat, but I couldn't see anything but gray sheets in front of me. If I couldn't see the boat, then nobody aboard would be able to see us. A few seconds later, in the distance—what appeared to be about two football fields away—was the bow of a boat rocking wildly in the sea.

I dropped back down to where Rachel and Rosalyn were waiting, and gave them the sign meaning "boat" and waved them to follow me. We stuck together.

People threw out towlines, and as the divers grabbed the lines we closed in on the boat. We were coughing and breathing hard, shivering from the wind, which had turned cold, and trying to explain what had happened.

We were safe and alive. It was that single experience underwater that made me realize the value of diving with people sharing the same bond, diving with people you trust to keep you calm through adversity, people you know would never leave you when nature suddenly changes all of your plans.

Jones indoctrinates his students with one central rule: *Never* leave your buddy.

The five-day meeting was drawing to a close. Mid-November was not the best time to take a three-and-a-half hour ride thirty-seven miles from shore in six-foot seas and blinding rain.

"We'll be back," Oswald whispered. "We'll be back and our ancestors will be waiting for us."

Two seasons had passed since we'd aborted our dive on the *Henrietta Marie*. It was now May 1993. Only ten people had been invited to Key West this time. We began to gather on the wooden dock shortly after 5:30 AM. The sun was just beginning to make its debut.

The crew was loading tanks and water and everyone was checking their gear for spare parts and making sure they brought along all their equipment. No one was going to miss this dive because of a ripped fin or a forgotten mask. Everyone was accounted for. It was time to shove off.

The sea was dead calm by the time we anchored on

New Ground Reef. The wind was still; there was no land in sight, just miles of dark blue ocean in all directions. On this day, the sea was flat as glass. I could have skipped a stone ninety miles and chased the trail of ripples to the shoreline of Cuba.

I closed my eyes for just a few seconds, and while the boat rocked easily in the breeze, I paused to ask God to bless our pilgrimage to this sacred site on the sea.

David Moore, a maritime archaeologist, slipped into his wet suit; Doc Jones sat across the deck, buckling his jacket. He spit into his mask—natural antifog solution—and pulled it over his face, giving David the thumbs-up sign. Within seconds, they rolled off the boat and splashed into the ocean. We watched their bubbles until they disappeared, speculating as to how long it would take them to locate the site.

Forty-five minutes had passed and we were getting anxious. Fifteen more minutes passed when I heard someone from the stern shout, "They're back!" Doc and David didn't say a word until they both sat down and pulled off their masks and fins, water falling from their heads.

"We didn't find it," David said. "It's all changed down there so much."

"We'll look at that map again, grab a sandwich, and give it another shot in an hour."

"We've waited all of our lives to get here," I said. "A few more minutes isn't going to make much of a difference."

Doc and David had finished eating and had reviewed their compass headings again. I heard two splashes, and they vanished under the sea.

We all figured it would be awhile before Doc and David returned. I claimed a piece of deck, stretched out on my back, and looked toward the sky. And then a loud noise echoed across the sea.

Toward the bow, Ric Powell, an ex-navy diver, was wearing his African *kufi* and blowing into a large pink conch shell, creating a sound that he believed would summon our lost ancestors. He was trying everything he could think of to ensure a peaceful and successful experience at sea.

As Ric blew into the conch shell, Howard Moss began to beat a leather-skinned drum and Gene Tinnie reached for a large tambourine. Within seconds, they were recreating the sound of Africa, playing music with instruments much like the ones that African people use to lift their spirits and send messages from village to village.

"We're calling our ancestors," Ric said. "We're letting them know we're here and that we understand their pain and suffering and thank them for the strength they have given us to survive."

"They're back!" someone shouted over the music.

"We found it!" David shouted as he climbed up the ladder into the boat.

They removed their gear and there was quiet celebration. The wreck site had been located, we knew we were on the site, and we were all anxious to go underwater.

Oswald asked each of us to stand in a tight circle and join hands.

"We are here today, members of the National Association of Black Scuba Divers, to pay tribute to millions of people—men, women, and children, black people, our people—who lost their lives during the Middle Passage. Many of these innocent people lost their lives in this ocean, and many lost their lives on this slave ship whose spirits lie below us."

Oswald hadn't finished his first sentence when the waves came.

From a dead calm, the sea shook and small swells appeared from nowhere. Waves slapped the bow, as if we were being acknowledged—or welcomed—by a phenom-enal force. We paused for several minutes, each of us spending a moment to offer a private prayer. The winds subsided and calm returned to the sea.

The water was gentle. Within a few seconds, we had slipped beneath the surface and were dodging half a dozen jellyfish at five feet.

As we descended past a depth of fifteen feet, I followed Doc's bubbles. We couldn't see more than ten feet in any direction. The site was strangely familiar. I felt a kinship, a welcoming of sorts, although I had never visited this wreckage before.

We were all floating just above Doc and Ric, who were holding on to each side of the monument, slowly guiding the one-ton memorial to a sandy patch on the ocean floor.

At thirty feet, I could see sand and thin strands of grass. Doc glanced at his compass as he and Ric positioned the monument to the east, facing Africa. When Africans were buried in the Americas, their families laid them to rest with their heads facing east toward their homeland. We believed the monument to our ancestors should also face Africa.

We hovered in the still of the ocean a few feet above the

weighty memorial, our bodies and our souls soothed by the sea. We shifted with the current and watched the concrete pledge of our appreciation pound the ocean floor, the silt swirling as the monument made its solid impression in the sand.

In teams of two, we toured the memorial, each of us reaching out to touch the hand of the brother next to him; all of us stopping to read the inscription etched into a bronze plaque and bolted into the concrete:

> Henrietta Marie: *In memory and recognition of the courage, pain, and suffering of enslaved African people. Speak her name and gently touch the souls of our ancestors.*

PETER WESTBROOK is the greatest American fencer of the twentieth century. He represented the United States six times at the Olympics, from 1976 to 1996, winning the bronze medal in 1984. He won the gold at the Pan-American Games of 1983 and 1995, and has held the title of United States saber champion thirteen times. Understanding the needs of inner-city youth from firsthand experience, he created the Peter Westbrook Foundation to teach life skills through the discipline of fencing. Four fencers on the 2004 U.S. Olympic team were African American students from the Westbrook Foundation—a testament to its founder's ceaseless striving for excellence.

In the Zone

My mother wanted me to fence. I thought she was out of her mind.

"I give you five dollar if you go try," she offered in broken English.

"Why *fencing*, Ma?" I asked. I didn't know anyone who fenced, and hardly even knew what fencing was. Still, five dollars in those days was more like having fifteen dollars in your pocket today, and my mother was offering me five dollars for every lesson I took! I quickly dropped all my resistance to that strange white sport and started fencing lessons immediately.

It was 1967, and I had just entered high school in Newark, New Jersey. It was a turbulent time in America. The streets of Newark were blazing. In my neighborhood people were smoking reefer, popping pills, and getting in and out of trouble with the law. I saw men, women, teenagers, and cops fighting. I'd seen people killed on the street. Knives, bottles, hatchets, and billy clubs were more familiar to me than kitchen appliances. Just to get into my house every afternoon felt like a battle. Competition was something I had learned at an early age. But fighting was something different: a survival tactic that came to me out of necessity.

My mother wanted me to take up a sport that would draw my focus away from the streets and the violence of ghetto life. She knew that fencing would expose me to people from different backgrounds. That quick thinking on her part must have stemmed from memories of her own upbringing. Mariko-san Wada could trace her ancestry to samurai warriors in the service of the Japanese emperor.

My mother was no stranger to violence, even before her arrival in America. At the end of World War II, when the Americans bombed Japan, eighteen-year-old Mariko saw her mother blown up in the streets of Kobe. Later, she saw her mother's corpse once again, heaped onto a pile of others in the back of a truck. These experiences left a deep emotional scar on Mariko that she would carry for the rest of her life.

There were many U.S. soldiers in Japan at the time, and Ulysses Jonathan Westbrook, my African American father, was one of them. I don't know the details of how my mother met my father, but I do know this: Mariko Wada met and fell in love with a handsome black American GI who was stationed in Kobe. I think that he must have represented another world to her—far away from the nightmare she had survived.

It was my great good fortune to have the kind of mother I did. She instilled so many essential values in my sister and me. She taught us that we should never give up in our endeavors. She would literally tell us not to cry, to work hard, to be ethical, and to fight to achieve our goals.

Essex Catholic High School was a predominantly white, all-boys school in northern Newark, two bus rides away from where we lived. Essex had a great athletic program. In addition to the usual programs like track, baseball, basketball, and football, the school had fencing.

My first fencing teacher was an Italian American medical doctor named Samuel D'ambola. Dr. D'ambola started me out with the saber instead of the foil. While the foil is considered a basic, all-purpose sword that is easiest for beginners to handle, the saber is a military sword that was favored by cavalry captains and pirates of the high seas. It is a distinctive-looking weapon with a slightly curved blade and a curved knuckle guard which extends from the hand guard to the base of the grip. The saber evolved out of the cutlass, and is predominantly a cutting and slashing weapon, the kind Zorro used for his "Z."

In saber fencing, the target area is everything from the hips on up, including the arms and the head. It's a freer style, more like jazz or modern dance. With the foil, on the other hand, the target area is the torso, excluding the arms and the head. You can only score with the tip of the blade, only with the point. No cutting, no slashing, only poking.

Foil fencing is very elegant, kind of like ballet, with less movement and much more control. There is also a weapon called an épée, which was originally a dueling sword. It is similar to a foil, only a bit heavier and stiffer, with a larger hand guard. In épée fencing, the target area is the whole body, from head to toes. The best fencers in the world specialize in only one weapon, and the saber felt just right for me.

I quickly became attached to saber fencing. Fencing satisfied my constant need to be quick with everything I did. Since I was already a fighter, fighting with a sword instead of with fists or sticks came naturally to me. I loved being able to prove myself in one-on-one combat, to see if I could physically, mentally, and emotionally destroy my opponent. I would try to demoralize him to see how much abuse he could take. Fencing was just like street boxing, only not as brutal. And here was a kind of fighting that my mother not only allowed, but actually encouraged.

Dr. D'ambola's training program was rigorous, and certainly kept me off the streets. We trained every day after school from 3:00 to 6:00 PM, and traveled to competitions up and down the East Coast. We had the number-one fencing program in the state of New Jersey, and hadn't lost a match in years. Winning brought me a feeling of acceptance that I never had before. While I didn't yet have the skills or the savvy I would acquire over the years, my raw talent, tough determination, fighting spirit, and sheer barbarism were enough to keep me winning.

Four years of high school fencing had earned me a full scholarship to New York University. NYU was a powerhouse in the world of college fencing, just as Essex was in the high school arena. There were so many superstars there, it was like a fencing dynasty. I felt honored and awed and afraid to be among them. I realized that back at Essex, I might have been the best fencer around, but I was like a big fish in a little pond. NYU was like a tributary that led out into the great ocean.

Every serious fencer has to have a fencing mentor, a personal coach. The form can only be perfected through countless hours of one-on-one training. The coaches at NYU, seeing my potential, suggested that I start training with Csaba Elthes, a Hungarian saberist at the New York Fencers Club who had a reputation as the best coach in the country.

Csaba had me training seven days a week, from four in the afternoon until nine or ten at night. We'd start with a one-hour lesson, followed by footwork practice. Then I'd spar with other fencers, simulating competitive matches. I'd play against as many other fencers as I could to develop my reflexes and to hone my instinct for knowing what approach to use. I learned that some people only like to attack, and some only like to defend. If I'm up against an attacker, I close the distance between us to maximize my advantage. If I'm up against a defensive player, I try to throw him by attacking him with a variety of moves.

Csaba believed in me and worked me like a dog. This Old World maestro put me on the road to championship fencing. Under his guidance, it wasn't long before I was reputed to be one of the best saberists in the country.

The odds of winning at the Olympics have always been stacked high against American fencers. Many people are not aware of the fact that in most other competing countries, Olympic fencers are strictly professionals. Generous salaries, special privileges, media attention, and other perks are lavished on them—in the same way that basketball, football, and baseball players are treated in the United States. In France, for instance, two-time Olympic fencing champion Jean-François Lamour was recently named Athlete of the Year, with all the glamour and glory that accompanies such an honor. In stark contrast, America's Olympic fencers are amateurs who hold down outside jobs, train in their spare time, and pay coaches out of their own pockets. Sadly, fencing has never caught on as a spectator sport here, and it has been next to impossible to find long-term corporate sponsors for individual fencers.

Therefore, I was grateful to have the advantage of competing in my home country during the 1984 Olympics. Being in America meant that four thousand people in the audience would be rooting for me and calling out my name.

When I walk onto the strip in Los Angeles for my final match against the Frenchman Hervé Granger-Veron, my adrenaline is pumping. One of us will receive a bronze medal, and I don't know if I can pull it off. I twist my left ankle during practice shortly before the Games. But I'm not looking for excuses. I am fully prepared. I can conjure up all my strength and skills, all the emotional and intellectual and spiritual tools I have, and use them in a positive manner, without fear.

As the match begins, I get the first touch [out of the necessary ten to win]. I get the second touch. I make it to four. My touches appear to me to be so skillful, so beautiful, that I say to myself, *I think I'm in the Zone, but I'm not sure. Let me not think about it.* A lot of athletes and psychologists talk about this peak performance level called "the Zone." I think of the Zone as a spiritual gift that allows me to operate on an almost supernatural level and to produce incredible results. I don't like to tell myself I'm in the Zone too quickly, because you can easily find out that you're not a hundredth of a second later—when you lose.

Sure enough, as soon as the thought crosses my mind, the Frenchman gets two points on me. But I snatch the game right back. Soon the score hits 5–2, 6–2, 7–2, and I realize for sure that I'm in the Zone. Now I know I can do anything, and anything will work. Still, the battle isn't over.

In 1984, saber [scoring] was still not electrified. Today, when you hit your opponent, a light goes on, but in those days I had to count on a European judge to raise his hand for me. Just think about that. When I hit this Frenchman, the Europeans officiating are his *friends*. They do not want to give the point to me. But I've learned over time not to let the judges' calls break my spirit. So when I hit the guy once, twice, and no hand goes up, I know I gotta do it four, five, six more times before that hand begrudgingly rises. I get another touch, and it's 8–2. Then he gets 8–3, and 8–4. Even as he is gaining, I know the game is mine. All I gotta do is keep riding the tide, keep going with it. I get 9–4, and I finish him off 10–4. The Frenchman falls to his knees crying.

I had finally learned how to work in the Zone. On that day, I was able to realize it, to feel it, to understand it, and to run with it. I capitalized on that supernatural feeling. The Frenchman was devastated and the audience was amazed. When I looked out at the crowd, I could see that the Hungarians, the Italians, and the rest of the Europeans had all turned around. They went from not wanting my win to happen, to being forced to say in their hearts and souls, *Bravo. Bravo.* That to me was incredible.

The moment they placed the Olympic bronze medal around my neck as I stood on the champion's podium, I was beaming with pride. Winning a medal in a sport dominated by Latin Americans and Europeans was not just a personal victory. It felt that I had won for all African Americans. I felt a tremendous pride for my people. Unfortunately, we still live in a social climate where if you are black or dark-skinned, you will encounter people who will hint or say outright that somehow you are not as capable as everybody else. Somehow you are disqualified from participating in things that most people take for granted. On that day, I proved those people to be dead wrong.

Winning also kindled in my chest a deep and abiding confidence in a higher spiritual reality. Because the odds against my winning a medal at the Olympics were so great, I was convinced that I had been tapped on my head from above. It proved to me that I could be granted further blessings and strengths to deal with whatever other obstacles I should encounter.

RUSSELL SIMMONS *oversees a sprawling business empire based on hip-hop culture. Def Jam Records, Def Comedy Jam, and Phat Farm clothing are just a few of the brand names he has developed and made famous. He combines an astute eye for original talent with an instinct for knowing what people want and need before they even know it. Simmons is an excellent example of his own belief that the energy that created black art and culture can be used to build competitive and successful black businesses. Working to increase political awareness, Simmons is chairman of the Hip-Hop Summit Action Network.*

Rush and Rap

When I was sixteen years old I almost killed somebody. His street name was Red, which he'd earned for his reddish yellow complexion and his nasty, devilish temper. Red had robbed me on 205th Street, which in 1973 was the drug supermarket of my Hollis, Queens, neighborhood. To support my taste for flashy clothes, I had been selling herb on 205th Street, just a few blocks from where my family lived.

Being robbed while selling drugs is an occupational hazard. And there was no embarrassment in being ripped off by Red—sticking up dealers on 205th Street was one of his criminal specialties. Still, there was a lingering question among my drug-dealing peers: If Russell sees Red, what's he gonna do? More than a question, it was a challenge— one I'd have no choice but to answer one way or another.

Well, the answer came two weeks after Red robbed me. He came back on the block, apparently in search of his next victim. But before Red could make a move, we spotted him, and all the dealers started chasing him. We ran after Red for two or three blocks before a gang of us cornered him in the backyard of a single-family home. One of my niggas threw him down. A couple of the dealers sucker-punched him. And then, as Red struggled, somebody handed me a gun. It was the first (and only) time I've held a gun with the intention to shoot. I must have looked ready to bust a cap in him, because suddenly Red broke free of the three guys holding him and started climbing the backyard fence. Everything slowed down for me—now I was in the middle of one of those unexpected, scary, life-or-death moments. I held up the .45, aimed at Red's back, and fired. My bullet sailed right over his head. The last I saw of Red were his feet swinging over the wall. I can still hear the voices of the dealers running through my head and feel the heat from the gun in my hand. It's a feeling I've never forgotten. I used to boast to all my drug-dealing homies that I'd just missed Red's ass and if I got another chance, I would've went up in him. But in my heart I knew missing Red was the best thing I ever did. The truth was that kid was just running toward a bullet anyway. Two weeks later Red and his brother were both killed in a botched liquor-store robbery. I guess the owner was a better shot than me.

Sounds like a lyric from a rap, right? Nah, it wasn't a song, it was my life. But it's the kind of real-life story that has inspired hip-hop's storytellers for over twenty years.

That hip-hop embraces tales like mine—stories of decisions and danger with deep moral and emotional consequences—is one of the reasons it's grown so popular and I've had one of the greatest jobs in the world.

My life has largely been about promoting the anger, style, aggression, and attitude of urban America to a worldwide audience. I have helped sell the culture of hip-hop by identifying, nurturing, and promoting artists—rappers, comics, designers—who can take life-defining moments and turn them into commercial products that, at their highest level, become objects of art.

There were no rap stars when I was a teenager. There were no movies starring rappers or clothing lines bearing their names, or, for that matter, books written by people involved with them. With the help of many I built the business of hip-hop from the ground up to a multibillion-dollar industry. There was no long-term vision then. We were all just making it up as we went along.

The New York City that created hip-hop wasn't the one we live in today. The Big Apple back in the mid-1970s wasn't the strictly policed, prosperous, yuppified place it is today. Even the school I started attending, City College of New York, in Harlem, was viewed as a symbol of what

was wrong with New York. City College had open enroll-
ment, which guaranteed every student in the city a shot at
college. This flooded the school with black, Latino, and
immigrant kids, something resented by the old alumni.

It was in the CCNY student lounge that I met Rudy
Topping, aka Rudy Spli, one of the most influential people in my life. It was Rudy who nicknamed me Rush and
got me into promoting shows. Rudy was attending City
College and received a form of financial aid where you got
a check for $600 every semester. Back then $600 for a college student was a lot of cash. People would get the check,
think they were rich, and stop going to classes. Aside from
collecting his checks, Rudy's main interest was working as
a promoter at Charles Gallery in Harlem. Calling him a
promoter may be overstating his original involvement,
since basically all Rudy did was give out flyers. Still, it allowed him to get into the club for free, which made his gig
attractive to me.

Hanging out with Rudy at Charles Gallery is what led
me to my first hip-hop experience. On this particular
night it was Easy G on the ones and twos, cutting up the
kinds of records kids were into uptown. But the real reve-
lation was the "world-famous" Eddie Cheeba rhyming to
get the crowd excited.

Most of what he performed were simple rhymes to get people to dance and make noise ("Somebody, anybody, everybody scream!"), plus lines about how fly he was. It wasn't a sophisticated rhyme flow by current standards. But hearing Cheeba made me feel I'd just witnessed the invention of the wheel.

Just as shooting at Red and missing let me know, happily, that I had no future in real crime, watching and hearing Cheeba had an equally powerful effect. I was standing there in a room full of peers—black and Hispanic college kids, partying and drinking—and it hit me: I wanted to be in this business. Just like that I saw how I could turn my life in another, better way. All the street entrepreneurship I'd learned selling herb, hawking fake cocaine, and staying out of jail, I decided to put into promoting music.

With Rudy as my partner, I started investing my hard-earned money into renting venues and negotiating with acts. Starting to promote was great for my spirit, though it had a terrible, ultimately fatal effect on my schoolwork.

Eventually I left City College in my senior year, just four or five credits short of a sociology degree. This really upset my father, who thought I was a fool. For a while there I felt like I was a failure in my father's eyes, which hurt a lot, but promoting felt right in my gut. My mother was always more open to my brothers Danny, Joey, and me pursuing a more nontraditional, entrepreneurial way.

Early in my promoting career I lost all the money I'd saved putting on a show no one came to. I came out to Hollis and no one would help me. My father just wanted me to go back to school and told me so. What could I say? I had no money. Then my mother went back in the house and came out with $2,000 in crisp $100 bills from her personal savings. It was that money that kept me afloat until Kurtis Blow broke and I entered the record business. That act of love and faith, which is what kept me in business at a key time, is my favorite memory of her.

In 1981 I was twenty-four years old and feeling a lot of pressure. Here I was with Kurtis Blow, an act that had two gold singles ("Christmas Rappin'" and "The Breaks") and who was getting booked on major tours. In the wake of that success my management company was signing new clients every week, as more rappers were recording and needed representation. At that time there were no other managers who knew or cared about hip-hop with any credibility in that community. And on top of that, I was producing records too.

Yet I didn't really know how to do some of the things I

had to. Everything was new, and there was no textbook. I was learning how to be a manager with every meeting, with every phone call. Often it was just a matter of learning to command respect, which comes with the confidence that you know what you're talking about.

The biggest challenge was dealing with concert promoters. Often we'd get beat. A lot of the promoters felt comfortable jerking us because they were sure we were gonna disappear.

Run-D.M.C. is the most important act in hip-hop history, and I'm proud to say their story began in my family's attic. When my older brother, Danny, moved out of the house, my little brother, Joey, and I used the attic as a recreation room. Joey was always interested in music, so when he was ten my father bought him a drum set. By twelve, Joey had moved on to working turntables. He'd be up in the attic cutting on the wheels of steel, and everybody who heard him knew immediately he was gifted. Kurtis had to have a protégé who played turntables—and that became my brother Joey, aka DJ Run. Kurtis used to rhyme in his stage show, "Fast as an exploding bullet from my gun / is my disco son / Run."

At age seventeen, his last year in high school, I put him

in the studio with two friends and he started making records. One friend, Darryl McDaniel, aka D.M.C., had gone to public school with Run, and they'd known each other all their lives. Like Run, he came up with hip-hop and his taste was totally street. He had zero tolerance for R&B. The group's third member, Jason Mizell, aka Jam Master Jay, was from Hollis. He'd known Run and D.M.C. for years.

They aspired to keep it real when that wasn't yet considered important in rap. With Run-D.M.C., we got our chance to go in a direction that truly reflected the b-boy attitude. With the 12-inch "It's Like That" backed with "Sucker MCs" we became real producers and, I believe, revolutionized the sound of hip-hop records.

After we'd cut Run-D.M.C.'s records, I signed Run-D.M.C. to the independent label Profile Records. At that time there was no major label supporting rap so we got the best deal we could. Profile was the best independent label at the time, which meant they might pay you a little bit instead of nothing at all. We signed a contract for ten points and an advance of $25,000 for the first Run-D.M.C. album. We spent $15,000 recording the album and split the remaining $10,000.

Despite some tension in our relationship with Profile over money, I can't say they were cheap. But the reason Run-D.M.C. succeeded was that those three had the will to live. Run-D.M.C. eventually made their money on the road. At their peak they were getting up to $100,000 a night, so they just kept touring. After we had a hit with "My Adidas," we negotiated with that German athletic wear company to give us a deal—at one point it was $1 million a year for three years. So they had very significant income outside Profile. In a way records were their calling card, while Run-D.M.C. paid their bills through these other activities.

Starting out, I always wanted to be in the building inside one of the big labels. During the early days of Blow and Run I used to do club promotion for PolyGram. It allowed me to meet a lot of the executives at the label. They had nice offices, gold records on the wall, and fat expense accounts. To a kid who a year or two before had been selling fake cocaine, working at a label looked great. But the people in the black music department looked at me—scruffy beard, Adidas sneakers, track suit, ghetto music—and didn't see me as corporate material.

Turned out I was lucky that they wouldn't let me in,

'cause everything worth knowing in this business happens outside the building. Eventually I got to know everybody who was a player because once I had a hot record they had to call me.

I learned there is a cycle to a hit record. The booking agencies and the concert promoters call to book you. Once on the road, you meet all the record retailers and learn their business when your act stops by to sign autographs. When the act does radio interviews in cities they perform in, you meet all the radio programmers. So on tour you learn retail, radio, marketing, and promotion. And, of course, all this information helps you grow as a manager.

All that stuff can't be learned inside a building, because when you work at a label you can only do one job at a time. The Fresh Fest tour was a triumph of being locked outside the building. It was a tour that put the boot to the ground for rap. Fans flocked to those concerts because of hit records. They saw Run-D.M.C., Whodini, Kurtis Blow, and the Fat Boys, as well as DJs and break dancers. When they left they were not only buyers of records and concert tickets, but fans of the culture.

It was on the Fresh Fest tour that Run-D.M.C. established their reputation. They were b-boys beyond belief. They wore sneakers when other rappers were rocking thigh-high boots like Rick James. They wore leather suits and hats when other rappers had on cowboy outfits, feathers, and studded jackets like heavy metal stars. Run-D.M.C. saw what was happening in the street and stayed true to it.

For kids who couldn't be super-strong or really hard-core, rappers and wrestlers acted out their fantasies for them. Some of the artists back then looked at rap as such a ghetto phenomenon that they felt the need to tone it down and make it slicker for the masses. Catering to a mass audience usually backfires. Instead the key thing is to stay in your lane, and if you are good enough and interesting enough, people move to you. That way you change the mainstream, and that's what Run-D.M.C. did, opening the door for the rest of the acts and culture to continue that process.

An old record of theirs sounds great right now. That's a good thing. It just shows that if you maintain your honesty and integrity, commercial success and longevity will follow. That's a lesson I could only have learned outside the building.

BELL HOOKS *is the pen name of Gloria Watkins, Ph.D., Distinguished Professor of English at City College of New York. A prolific author, hooks is an outspoken intellectual committed to the liberation of black people and especially black women. She grew up feeling like a misfit, the problem child in a family of seven children in Kentucky. Her early independence and fearless insights often brought pain. But these same qualities also helped her create a voice that probes the inequities of American society with clarity and compassion. She adopted the name of her maternal great-grandmother, a Native American named Bell Hooks, though she spells it in lower-case letters—a symbol, she says, that the substance of her books is more important than the author.*

The Cave

His smells fill my nostrils with the scent of happiness. With him all the broken pieces of my heart get mended, put together again bit by bit. He can always tell when I am sad. He will ask me What have they been doing to you now. He knows that I am a wounded animal, that they pour salt on the open sores just to hear me moan. He tells me that in the end it will come out all right. He tells me Blessed are they that mourn for they shall be comforted. I am comforted by his presence. Soot-black-skinned man with lines etched deep in his face as if someone took a knife and carved them there.

He is Daddy Gus, mama's father. From her I know that he has always been gentle, that he has never been a man of harsh words. I need his presence in my life to learn that all men are not terrible, are not to be feared. He, too, is one of the faithful, one of the right-hand men of god. When he speaks I listen very carefully to hear what is said. His voice comes from some secret place of knowing, a hidden cave where the healers go to hear messages from the beloved.

In my dream we run away together, hand in hand. We go to the cave. To enter we must first remove all our clothes, we must wash, we must rub our body with a red mud. We cover ourselves so completely that we are no longer recognizable as grandfather and granddaughter. We enter without family ties or memory. The cave is covered with paintings that describe the way each animal has come to know that inside all of us is a place for healing, that we have only to discover it. Each animal searches and searches until they find the opening of the cave. As soon as they enter, the mind ceases, they feel at peace. They feel they are no longer blind, that they see for the first time. It is too much for the heart to bear. They stand together weeping, sobbing.

When we enter the cave we also take the time to weep, to lose ourselves in sorrow. We make a fire. In the fire are all the lost spirits that show us ways to live in the world. I do not yet have a language with which to speak with them. He knows. He speaks. I am the silent one, the one who bears witness. In the dream we leave the cave in quiet. Just as we reach the outside he begins talking to me without opening his mouth. He places his voice inside my head, telling me that knowledge of the cave can be given to anyone, only they must be seeking, that until I can tell a seeker from someone who is just curious I must not speak about it.

We are again grandfather and granddaughter. My visits to him are frequent. He has a favorite chair by the stove in the living room. When I was much smaller I sat there cuddled in his lap like a cat, hardly moving, hardly alive so near to the stillness of death was the bliss I knew in his arms. His room is filled with treasures. Once the curtain has been drawn at the doorway so that the others cannot see, he tells me that everything has life, a tiny soul inside it—things like pocketknives, coins, bits of ribbon. He is always finding the treasures people have lost or abandoned. He hears their small souls crying in the wilderness. He gives them a place to rest.

In his room treasures are everywhere. Every object has a story. He teaches me to listen to the stories things tell, to appreciate their history. He has many notebooks, little black notebooks filled with faded yellow paper. I understand from him that the notebooks are a place for the storage of memory. He writes with a secret pencil; the pages seem covered in ash, the ash left by the fire we have visited. This fire he says now burns inside us.

There is much to celebrate about being old. I want to be old as soon as possible for I see the way the old ones live—free. They are free to be different—unique—

distinct from one another. None of them are alike. Some of them were already on their way to being old when I was born. I do not know them young. I do not have to forgive them past mistakes. They have not caused me any sorrow. My grandfather tells me that all he ever wanted was for the world to leave him be, that it won't let you be when you are a young man. The world demands that you work for it, make families, provide, take no time to listen to your own heart beating.

He tells me that he could not accept much of what the world had to offer men, especially the business of going to war. All his sons who became soldiers lost parts of themselves. He tells me that there is no way one can kill another and not lose part of oneself. He tells me that he would not go to war, that he refused to fight. I want to know the details, why was he not drafted, why did no one force him to serve. He is indignant that I would suggest he could be forced to do anything against his will. He tells me that no one can make you do anything against your will.

The people in this house think of him as a coward, a small man shrinking into his chair like a shadow. They make fun of him, of his clothes, of his habits. They think all his treasures are junk. They have never heard their hearts beating. He has heard his—hearing this sound above all other sounds he is not provoked by their endless ridicule or attack. Sometimes in the midst of it all he reaches for his hat. He moves toward the door slowly, not even suggesting by a hurried walk that he has had enough. They do not follow him.

He is a man who does odd jobs. He works mainly for white folks, retired ladies who come out of their houses and speak to him as if he was ten years old, demanding that he cut the yard, empty their trash. He never looks them in the face. He never pays them any mind. They are he says only ghosts. He does not believe in ghosts. He works slowly, the sound of his heart setting the rhythm.

The day that his odd job is to burn trash in a nearby white lady's yard he feels tired and uncertain. The wind blows. He knows it is not a good day to burn trash but he does so anyway. He listens to his heart, beating unsteady, beating out a new rhythm. He knows that his end is near. He will not fight death. He has never been a soldier. He will give himself over to it freely. When the flames reach his body he does not notice. He does not smell the burning clothes. He has lost all memory. He has entered the cave.

She notices—Miss White Lady. She notices that in her

backyard an old man with a face like soot is surrounded in flames. She panics, not knowing who she can call to meet the needs of an old black man on fire. She calls his home. A grandchild comes running, jumps high fences, breaks bushes, puts out the flames with his hands. These are love's hands. They can do anything. He has heard the sound of this old man's heart beating. He has been comforted by his presence. In this moment he is able to fully return that love. He will never know such honor again.

They must travel many miles to the hospital where burns are treated. Those who love him sit nearby listening to his heart. A person on fire often dies not from the flames but from a heart attack as the pain is so intense. His heart does not fail him. It knows the fire is not his enemy. I know there is a secret in the flames that is ongoing and everlasting.

I cannot stand the hiding. I cannot stand all the secret places I have had to make inside myself.

I have discovered paint. Mixing the water with the powder makes color bright and primary. I imagine that I have returned to the cave of my childhood dreams, to the paintings on the wall. The art teacher, Mr. Harold, watches me stirring. He tells me he has been watching me since class began, that he enjoys the sight of a student falling in love with color again and again. He brings me a stack of paper. I wait always before I begin painting. He says I take too long, that such intense concentration may block the creativity. I want him to leave me alone. I am silent. He understands. He will come back later. I am trying to remember the pictures in the cave, the animals. If I can paint them all I am sure I can discover again the secret of living, what it was I left in the cave. I start with the color black. In a book on the history of pigments I come across a new phrase, bone black. Bone black is a black carbonaceous substance obtained by calcifying bones in closed vessels. Burning bones, that's what it makes me think about—flesh on fire, turning black, turning into ash.

I begin with the mouth of the cave, add red to the black. The red is the heart of the seekers, the animals and human beings who come. The next picture is one of the fire. Up close, with outstretched hands feeling the warmth, I remember that the fire is not just the color red, that it is blue and yellow and green. These are the colors of the lost spirits. Mixed together they bring new life to color. At the bottom of the fire is the color black. This is the ash that the fire becomes. This is the remains of all the animals who have given their life in sacrifice to keep the spirit moving, burning bright.

I want to make the color gray, to paint a world covered in mist, but this painting must wait, for it is what I see when I leave the cave. The animals must be painted. I try and try but cannot get them right. Mr. Harold looks at me from his desk and says no as he sees me about to rip the paper, to throw it away. He shakes his head, no. He has told me many times to keep at it, to look at it, to rethink what it is I am trying to do.

Loneliness brings me to the edge of what I know. My soul is dark like the inner world of the cave—bone black. I have been drowning in that blackness. Like quicksand it sucks me in and keeps me there in the space of all my pain. I never say out loud that I could die in this space of loneliness, of outsiderness. I never tell anyone how much I want to belong.

I read poems. I write. That is my destiny. Standing on the edge of the cliff about to fall into the abyss, I remember who I am. I am a young poet, a writer. I am here to make words. I have the power to pull myself back from death—to keep myself alive. Now when they tell me I am crazy, that if I keep reading all those books I will end up crazy, locked away in the asylum where no one will visit me—now when they tell me this I am not so afraid. Rilke gives meaning to the wilderness of spirit I am living in. He tells me that everything terrible is really something helpless that wants help from us. I read his *Letters to a Young Poet* over and over. I am drowning and it is the raft that takes me safely to shore.

Now when I lie in bed at night thinking that it is better to die than always to be misunderstood, always to feel so much pain, I know that I am not alone. Lying in the dark I repeat the words, "Do not believe that he who would seek to comfort you lives untroubled." I still suffer. Daddy Gus says that my suffering will end. That one day I will look back on all of this and it will not matter.

I take my book to read him passages. Like Rilke, he tells me not to be afraid to look deep into everything, not to be afraid even of the pain. I can tell him, my grandfather who loves me always, that I want to belong—that it hurts to be always on the outside. He tells me there are lots of ways to belong in this world. And that it is my work to find out where I belong.

In my journal I write—I belong in this place of words. This is my home. This dark, bone black inner cave where I am making a world for myself.

NEIL DEGRASSE TYSON *is director of the Hayden Planetarium in New York City, the youngest person ever named to that position. He is also an astrophysicist at the American Museum of Natural History. His research interests include star formation, exploding stars, dwarf galaxies, and the structure of the Milky Way, the galaxy of about 100 billion stars that includes our solar system. While Dr. Tyson specializes in one of the most complex areas of science, he has the vital gift of clarity. He makes tough ideas easy to understand as he brings his passion for studying the universe down to earth.*

Stargazer

It was a dark and starry night. I felt as though I could see forever. Too numerous to count, the stars of the autumn sky, and the constellations they trace, were rising slowly in the east while the waxing crescent moon was descending into the western horizon. Aloft in the northern sky were the Big and Little Dippers, just where they were described to be, just as they were described to appear. The planets Jupiter and Saturn were high in the sky. One of the stars seemed to fall toward the horizon. It was a meteor streaking through the atmosphere. I was told there would be no clouds that night, but I saw one. It was long and skinny and stretched across the sky from horizon to horizon. No, I was mistaken. It wasn't a cloud. It was the Milky Way. I had never seen the sky of the Milky Way with such clarity and majesty as that night.

Forty-five minutes swiftly passed when the house lights came back on in the planetarium sky theater.

That was the night. The night the universe poured down from the sky and flowed into my body. I had been called. The study of the universe would be my career, and no force on Earth would stop me. I was just nine years old, but I now had an answer for that perennially annoying question all adults ask: "What do you want to be when you grow up?" Although I could barely pronounce the word, I would tell them, "I want to be an astrophysicist."

From that moment onward, one question lingered within me: Was this majestic planetarium sky an accurate portrayal of the real celestial sphere? Or was it a hoax? Surely there were too many stars. I had proof because I had seen the night sky from the Bronx—from the rooftop of my apartment house. Built upon one of the highest hills of the borough, it was one of a set of three buildings twenty-two stories high that were prophetically known as the Skyview Apartments.

In one of the other Skyview buildings lived a close friend—a classmate in elementary school. He taught me to play chess, poker, pinochle, Risk, and Monopoly. He introduced me to brainteaser books. The more we played, the more stretched and sharpened my brain became.

My friend's most important contribution to my life's path, however, was introducing me to binoculars. I had used them before—primarily to view sporting events and to look into other people's windows. My friend instead encouraged me to look up, beyond the streetlights, beyond the buildings, beyond the clouds, and out toward the Moon and stars of the night sky.

The Moon through those 7x35s was not just bigger, it was better. The coal-dark shadows sharply revealed its surface to be three-dimensional—a rich moonscape of mountains and valleys and craters and hills and plains. The Moon was no longer just a thing on the sky—it was another world in the universe. And if simple binoculars could transform the Moon, imagine what mountaintop telescopes could do with the rest of the universe.

Galileo was the first person in the world to look up with a good enough telescope to see what no one before him had ever dreamed: structure on the lunar surface, revolving spots on the Sun, the phases of Venus (just like the Moon), Saturn and its rings, Jupiter and its restless moons, and stars composing the faint glow of the Milky Way. My discoveries, although old news for society, were no less astonishing for me than they must have been for Galileo in 1610.

My sixth-grade homeroom and science teacher was Mrs. Susan Kreindler, who was a tall woman with a keen sense of academic discipline. For the third quarter of my sixth-grade report card she wrote, "Less social involvement and more academic diligence is in order!"

Mrs. Kreindler clipped a small advertisement from the newspaper announcing astronomy courses at the Hayden

Planetarium. One of them was called "Astronomy for Young People." She recommended that I explore them. From then onward, the Hayden Planetarium became a much broader and deeper resource to the growth of my life's interests. I had previously known it only to be a place with a beautiful night sky—but I came to learn that the actual universe is much, much bigger.

A student's academic life experience can be constructed from much more than what happens in a classroom. Good teachers know this. The best teachers make sure it happens.

My love affair with the universe was in the fast lane, with my interests soon outstripping my first telescope's power. All other things being equal, bigger telescopes are better than smaller telescopes. Unlike what you might be told in other sectors of life, when observing the universe, size does matter, which often leads to polite "telescope envy." Larger telescopes simply gather more light and see dimmer things. I received no weekly or monthly allowance from my parents. Expensive acquisitions required a job.

I bought my six-inch Newtonian reflecting telescope from monies earned by walking other people's dogs. These weren't ordinary dogs. These were apartment-dwelling city dogs, not to be confused with the streetwise variety. I walked large ones, small ones, mean ones, and friendly ones. But what they all had in common was disdain for inclement weather and a strong preference for taking the elevator over walking up or down the stairs. Going outside was a distraction from their warm and dry apartment life. Most dogs had raincoats. Some had hats and booties. I earned fifty cents per dog, per walk, during all my years in junior high school—enough to pay for two-thirds of both my telescope and an entry-level Pentax SLR 35 mm camera, equipped with specialized adapters for astrophotography. My parents kicked in the rest.

With its five-foot-long white tube, mounted with counterweights on a heavy-duty metal pier, my telescope looked like a cross between an artillery cannon and a grenade launcher. Like most telescopes above a certain cost, mine was equipped with an electric clock drive that compensated for Earth's rotation by tracking the motion of stars across the sky. The roof of my building had no power outlets, but my dentist (a lifelong friend of the family) happened to live on the nineteenth floor. I would faithfully haul to the roof, along with my telescope, a hundred-foot heavy-duty extension cord and lower it into the bedroom window of his apartment.

I was simply reaching out to the universe. As for nosy

neighbors, my rooftop activities looked to them as though I were a heavily armed cat burglar, ready to rappel down the side of the apartment building in the dark, with my portable assault weapons strapped to my side. A third of the time I was on the roof, someone would call the police.

Whatever had been said of police officers, I have yet to meet one who was not impressed by the sight of the Moon, planets, or stars through a telescope. Saturn alone bailed me out a half-dozen times. For all I know, I would have been shot to death on numerous occasions were it not for the majesty of the night sky.

Of all the planets in the sky, my favorite is Saturn. Without question, debate, or argument, Saturn is the most beautiful. Saturn was also the first planet that I ever saw through my first telescope. Imagine the thrill of first locating a point of light on the sky. Then centering it in the crosshairs of a finder scope and looking through the telescope's eyepiece to reveal another world—a celestial orb surrounded by a ring system three times the width of the planet itself. Several moons are clearly visible through a simple telescope, but at last count twenty or so are catalogued.

One of the projects in my seventh-grade woodworking

shop was to make a lamp. I decided to craft one of my own design. My wooden lamp would have a cosmic theme designed after a planet. My wooden lamp would be Saturn. In my design the light bulb housing emerged from the top of a white pine sphere about nine inches in diameter. Two dowels emerged from the equator of the ball to support a broad mahogany ring that tilted on the dowels. With the lamp's chain connected from the base of the bulb housing to the ring's edge, the lamp could be turned on and off by tilting Saturn's ring. A wooden pedestal supported the ball from below, with a layer of felt underneath to protect the furniture on which it rested.

I got an A+, and it remains my primary desk lamp today.

I enjoyed another encounter with Saturn while on board the SS *Canberra* on the way back from viewing the total solar eclipse of June 30, 1973* off the coast of northwest Africa. This particular Cunard luxury liner had been converted to a floating scientific laboratory where all manner of astrophysical experiments were conducted

---

* July 1973 coincided with the five-hundredth anniversary of the birth of the Polish astronomer Nicolaus Copernicus, the father of the Sun-centered model of the universe.

during the seven minutes of blocked sunlight—one of the longest eclipses on record. I had received a small scholarship from the Explorers Club of New York to take this trip alone. At age fourteen, I was the youngest unaccompanied person on the boat, but I had my telescope in tow, which was all the guardianship I needed.

Two thousand scientists, engineers, and eclipse enthusiasts were onboard, as well as assorted luminaries such as the astronauts Neil Armstrong and Scott Carpenter. The prolific Dr. Isaac Asimov was also onboard. He gave a thoroughly entertaining and informative lecture on the history of eclipses. I was a lucky guy.

In addition to the dozens of educational lectures and presentations, the journey home included fun intellectual diversions such as an astronomy trivia contest, where my knowledge of Saturn happened to matter greatly. With about fifty contestants, teamed in tables of four or five, a master of ceremonies started asking all manner of questions about the cosmos. Successions of hard questions swiftly eliminated many tables. One question stumped everyone. "Which day of the year can never have a total solar eclipse?" The correct answer was Easter, which is defined to fall on the first Sunday after the first full moon after the first day of spring in the Northern Hemisphere. Easter therefore falls, at most, seven days after the full moon, while total solar eclipses can happen only during the moment of the new moon, which falls a full two weeks away from the full moon. I grew to learn that practically any Moon-based holiday that did not specify the astronomical new moon would also qualify as a correct answer, such as Good Friday, Passover, Ramadan, and the Chinese New Year.

Another question that stumped and therefore eliminated a bunch of tables was "What are the linguistically correct names for objects or aliens from Mars, Venus, and Jupiter?" I knew this one cold. While everybody knew that aliens from Mars are called Martians, fewer people knew that aliens from Jupiter are called Jovians. And only a handful of people knew that aliens from Venus are called Venereals. The word *Venereal* is not in common use among astronomers, in favor of the less contagious-sounding *Venutian*. Blame the medical community. Venus is the goddess of love and beauty, so I suppose she ought to be the goddess of its medical consequences.

At the end of the contest, two tables remained in the running, including mine. The final question was "What feature of Saturn, other than its beautiful ring system, strongly distinguishes it from all other planets in the solar system?" I knew that my Saturn lamp (from seventh-grade shop class) would float if you tossed it into a bathtub because it was made of wood and wood is less dense than water. So too would the planet Saturn float if you could find a bathtub big enough to place it. Saturn is the only planet whose average density is less than that of water. I stood up before the assemblage and delivered the winning answer. For that bit of trivia I earned applause from everyone in the room and a free bottle of champagne for my table. Having gazed so long at the stars, I now had my first taste of being one—if only for a brief but sparkling moment.